Defoe Abbott Marx Hardy Montaigne Machiavelli Haggard Chesterton Cooper Emerson Joyce Austen Hugo Eliot Grimm

Melville Carroll Christie Maupassant Byron Molière Schiller

Stoker Wilde Garnett Einstein Fitzgerald Hawthorne Smith Kafka Hall

Goethe Dostoyevsky Willis

Cotton Kipling Doyle

Baum Henry Nietzsche Balzac

Leslie Dumas Flaubert Turgenev Vatsyayana Crane

Stockton Verne

Burroughs Vinci

Curtis Tocqueville Gogol Busch

Homer Widger Tolstoy Whitman

Darwin Thoreau Twain Scott

Potter Freud Zola Plato Harte

Kant Jowett Lawrence Dickens Burton Hesse

Andersen Cervantes

London Descartes Voltaire

Poe Aristotle Wells Cooke

Hale James Hastings

Bunner Shakespeare Irving

Richter Chambers

Doré Dante Chekhov Shaw Wodehouse Benedict Alcott

Swift da Pushkin Newton

Castilian Days

John Hay

Imprint

This book is part of TREDITION CLASSICS

Author: John Hay
Cover design: Buchgut, Berlin – Germany

Publisher: tredition GmbH, Hamburg - Germany
ISBN: 978-3-8424-3023-5

www.tredition.com
www.tredition.de

CASTILIAN DAYS

BY JOHN HAY

PUBLISHERS' NOTE

In this Holiday Edition of *Castilian Days* it has been thought advisable to omit a few chapters that appeared in the original edition. These chapters were less descriptive than the rest of the book, and not so rich in the picturesque material which the art of the illustrator demands. Otherwise, the text is reprinted without change. The illustrations are the fruit of a special visit which Mr. Pennell has recently made to Castile for this purpose.

BOSTON, AUTUMN, 1903

CONTENTS

MADRID AL FRESCO

Madrid is a capital with malice aforethought. Usually the seat of government is established in some important town from the force of circumstances. Some cities have an attraction too powerful for the court to resist. There is no capital of England possible but London. Paris is the heart of France. Rome is the predestined capital of Italy in spite of the wandering flirtations its varying governments in different centuries have carried on with Ravenna, or Naples, or Florence. You can imagine no Residenz for Austria but the Kaiserstadt, — the gemuthlich Wien. But there are other capitals where men have arranged things and consequently bungled them. The great Czar Peter slapped his imperial court down on the marshy shore of the Neva, where he could look westward into civilization and watch with the jealous eye of an intelligent barbarian the doings of his betters. Washington is another specimen of the cold-blooded handiwork of the capital builders. We shall think nothing less of the *clarum et venerabile nomen* of its founder if we admit he was human, and his wishing the seat of government nearer to Mount Vernon than Mount Washington sufficiently proves this. But Madrid more plainly than any other capital shows the traces of having been set down and properly brought up by the strong hand of a paternal government; and like children with whom the same regimen has been followed, it presents in its maturity a curious mixture of lawlessness and insipidity.

Its greatness was thrust upon it by Philip II. Some premonitory symptoms of the dangerous honor that awaited it had been seen in preceding reigns. Ferdinand and Isabella occasionally set up their pilgrim tabernacle on the declivity that overhangs the Manzanares. Charles V. found the thin, fine air comforting to his gouty articulations. But Philip II. made it his court. It seems hard to conceive how a king who had his choice of Lisbon, with its glorious harbor and unequalled communications; Seville, with its delicious climate and natural beauty; and Salamanca and Toledo, with their wealth of tradition, splendor of architecture, and renown of learning, should have chosen this barren mountain for his home, and the seat of his empire. But when we know this monkish king we wonder no longer. He chose Madrid simply because it was cheerless and bare and of ophthalmic ugliness. The royal kill-joy delighted in having the dreariest capital on earth. After a while there seemed to him too much life and humanity about Madrid, and he built the Escorial, the grandest ideal of majesty and ennui that the world has ever seen. This vast mass of granite has somehow acted as an anchor that has held the capital fast moored at Madrid through all succeeding years.

It was a dreary and somewhat shabby court for many reigns. The great kings who started the Austrian dynasty were too busy in their world conquest to pay much attention to beautifying Madrid, and their weak successors, sunk in ignoble pleasures, had not energy enough to indulge the royal folly of building. When the Bourbons came down from France there was a little flurry of construction under Philip V., but he never finished his palace in the Plaza del Oriente, and was soon absorbed in constructing his castle in cloud-land on the heights of La Granja. The only real ruler the Bourbons ever gave to Spain was Charles III., and to him Madrid owes all that it has of architecture and civic improvement. Seconded by his able and liberal minister, Count Aranda, who was educated abroad, and so free from the trammels of Spanish ignorance and superstition, he rapidly changed the ignoble town into something like a city. The greater portion of the public buildings date from this active and beneficent reign. It was he who laid out the walks and promenades which give to Madrid almost its only outward attraction. The Picture Gallery, which is the shrine of all pilgrims of taste, was built by him for a Museum of Natural Science. In nearly all that a stranger cares to see, Madrid is not an older city than Boston.

There is consequently no glory of tradition here. There are no cathedrals. There are no ruins. There is none of that mysterious and haunting memory that peoples the air with spectres in quiet towns like Ravenna and Nuremberg. And there is little of that vast movement of humanity that possesses and bewilders you in San Francisco and New York. Madrid is larger than Chicago; but Chicago is a great city and Madrid a great village. The pulsations of life in the two places resemble each other no more than the beating of Dexter's heart on the home-stretch is like the rising and falling of an oozy tide in a marshy inlet.

There is nothing indigenous in Madrid. There is no marked local color. It is a city of Castile, but not a Castilian city, like Toledo, which girds its graceful waist with the golden Tagus, or like Segovia, fastened to its rock in hopeless shipwreck.

But it is not for this reason destitute of an interest of its own. By reason of its exceptional history and character it is the best point in Spain to study Spanish life. It has no distinctive traits itself, but it is a patchwork of all Spain. Every province of the Peninsula sends a contingent to its population. The Gallicians hew its wood and draw its water; the Asturian women nurse its babies at their deep bosoms, and fill the promenades with their brilliant costumes; the Valentians carpet its halls and quench its thirst with orgeat of chufas; in every street you shall see the red bonnet and sandalled feet of the Catalan; in every cafe, the shaven face and rat-tail chignon of the Majo of Andalusia. If it have no character of its own, it is a mirror where all the faces of the Peninsula may sometimes be seen. It is like the mockingbird of the West, that has no song of its own, and yet makes the woods ring with every note it has ever heard.

Though Madrid gives a picture in little of all Spain, it is not all Spanish. It has a large foreign population. Not only its immediate neighbors, the French, are here in great numbers,—conquering so far their repugnance to emigration, and living as gayly as possible in the midst of traditional hatred,—but there are also many Germans and English in business here, and a few stray Yankees have pitched their tents, to reinforce the teeth of the Dons, and to sell them ploughs and sewing-machines. Its railroads have waked it up to a new life, and the Revolution has set free the thought of its people to an extent which would have been hardly credible a few years ago. Its streets swarm with newsboys and strangers,—the agencies that are to bring its people into the movement of the age.

It has a superb opera-house, which might as well be in Naples, for all the national character it has; the court theatre, where not a word of Cas-tilian is ever heard, nor a strain of Spanish music. Even cosmopolite Paris has her grand opera sung in French, and easy-going Vienna insists that Don Juan shall make love in German. The champagny strains of Offenbach are heard in every town of Spain oftener than the ballads of the country. In Madrid there are more *pilluelos* who whistle *Bu qui s'avance* than the Hymn of Riego. The Cancan has taken its place on the boards of every stage in the city, apparently to stay; and the exquisite jota and cachucha are giving way to the bestialities of the casino cadet. It is useless perhaps to fight against that hideous orgie of vulgar Menads which in these late years has swept over all nations, and stung the loose world into a tarantula dance from the Golden Horn to the Golden Gate. It must have its day and go out; and when it has passed, perhaps we may see that it was not so utterly causeless and irrational as it seemed; but that, as a young American poet has impressively said, "Paris was proclaiming to the world in it somewhat of the pent-up fire and fury of her nature, the bitterness of her heart, the fierceness of her protest against spiritual and political repression. It is an execration in rhythm, — a dance of fiends, which Paris has invented to express in license what she lacks in liberty."

This diluted European, rather than Spanish, spirit may be seen in most of the amusements of the politer world of Madrid. They have classical concerts in the circuses and popular music in the open air. The theatres play translations of French plays, which are pretty good when they are in prose, and pretty dismal when they are turned into verse, as is more frequent, for the Spanish mind delights in the jingle of rhyme. The fine old Spanish drama is vanishing day by day. The masterpieces of Lope and Calderon, which inspired all subsequent playwriting in Europe, have sunk almost utterly into oblivion. The stage is flooded with the washings of the Boulevards. Bad as the translations are, the imitations are worse. The original plays produced by the geniuses of the Spanish Academy, for which they are crowned and sonneted and pensioned, are of the kind upon which we are told that gods and men and columns look austerely.

This infection of foreign manners has completely gained and now controls what is called the best society of Madrid. A soiree in this circle is like an evening in the corresponding grade of position in Paris or Petersburg or New York in all external characteristics. The toilets are by Worth; the beauties are coiffed by the deft fingers of Parisian tiring-women; the men wear the penitential garb of Poole; the music is by Gounod and Verdi; Strauss inspires the rushing waltzes, and the married people walk through the quadrilles to the measures of Blue Beard and Fair Helen, so suggestive of conjugal rights and duties. As for the suppers, the trail of the Neapolitan serpent is over them all. Honest eating is a lost art among the effete denizens of the Old World. Tantalizing ices, crisped shapes of baked nothing, arid sandwiches, and the feeblest of sugary punch, are the only supports exhausted nature receives for the shock of the cotillon. I remember the stern reply of a friend of mine when I asked him to go with me to a brilliant reception, — "No! Man liveth not by biscuit-glace alone!" His heart was heavy for the steamed cherry-stones of Harvey and the stewed terrapin of Augustin.

The speech of the gay world has almost ceased to be national. Every one speaks French sufficiently for all social requirements. It is sometimes to be doubted whether this constant use of a foreign language in official and diplomatic circles is a cause or effect of paucity of ideas. It is impossible for any one to use another tongue with the ease and grace with which he could use his own. You know how tiresome the most charming foreigners are when they speak English. A fetter-dance is always more curious than graceful. Yet one who has nothing to say can say it better in a foreign language. If you must speak nothing but phrases, Ollendorff's are as good as any one's. Where there are a dozen people all speaking French equally badly, each one imagines there is a certain elegance in the hackneyed forms. I know of no other way of accounting for the fact that clever people seem stupid and stupid people clever when they speak French. This facile language thus becomes the missionary of mental equality, — the principles of '89 applied to conversation. All men are equal before the phrase-book.

But this is hypercritical and ungrateful. We do not go to balls to hear sermons nor discuss the origin of matter. If the young grandees of Spain are rather weaker in the parapet than is allowed in the nineteenth century, if the old boys are more frivolous than is becoming to age, and both more ignorant of the day's doings than is consistent with even their social responsibilities, in compensation the women of this circle are as pretty and amiable as it is possible to be in a fallen world. The foreigner never forgets those piquant, *mutines* faces of Andalusia and those dreamy eyes of Malaga, — the black masses of Moorish hair and the blond glory of those graceful heads that trace their descent from Gothic demigods. They were not very learned nor very witty, but they were knowing enough to trouble the soundest sleep. Their voices could interpret the sublimest ideas of Mendelssohn. They knew sufficiently of lines and colors to dress themselves charmingly at small cost, and their little feet were well enough educated to bear them over the polished floor of a ball-room as lightly as swallows' wings. The flirting of their intelligent fans, the flashing of those quick smiles where eyes, teeth, and lips all did their dazzling duty, and the satin twinkling of those neat boots in the waltz, are harder to forget than things better worth remembering.

Since the beginning of the Revolutionary regime there have been serious schisms and heart-burnings in the gay world. The people of the old situation assumed that the people of the new were rebels and traitors, and stopped breaking bread with them. But in spite of this the palace and the ministry of war were gay enough,—for Madrid is a city of office-holders, and the White House is always easy to fill, even if two thirds of the Senate is uncongenial. The principal fortress of the post was the palace of the spirituelle and hospitable lady whose society name is Duchess of Penaranda, but who is better known as the mother of the Empress of the French. Her salon was the weekly rendezvous of the irreconcilable adherents of the House of Bourbon, and the aristocratic beauty that gathered there was too powerful a seduction even for the young and hopeful partisans of the powers that be. There was nothing exclusive about this elegant hospitality. Beauty and good manners have always been a passport there. I have seen a proconsul of Prim talking with a Carlist leader, and a fiery young democrat dancing with a countess of Castile.

But there is another phase of society in Madrid which is altogether pleasing,—far from the domain of politics or public affairs, where there is no pretension or luxury or conspiracy,—the old-fashioned Tertulias of Spain. There is nowhere a kindlier and more unaffected sociableness. The leading families of each little circle have one evening a week on which they remain at home. Nearly all their friends come in on that evening. There is conversation and music and dancing. The young girls gather together in little groups,—not confined under the jealous guard of their mothers or chaperons,—and chatter of the momentous events of the week—their dresses, their beaux, and their books. Around these compact formations of loveliness skirmish light bodies of the male enemy, but rarely effect a lodgment. A word or a smile is momently thrown out to meet the advance; but the long, desperate battle of flirtation, which so often takes place in America in discreet corners and outlying boudoirs, is never seen in this well-organized society. The mothers in Israel are ranged for the evening around the walls in comfortable chairs, which they never leave; and the colonels and generals and chiefs of administration, who form the bulk of all Madrid gatherings, are gravely smoking in the library or playing interminable games of tresillon, seasoned with temperate denunciations of the follies of the time.

Nothing can be more engaging than the tone of perfect ease and cordial courtesy which pervades these family festivals. It is here that the Spanish character is seen in its most attractive light. Nearly everybody knows French, but it is never spoken. The exquisite Castilian, softened by its graceful diminutives into a rival of the Italian in tender melody, is the only medium of conversation; it is rare that a stranger' is seen, but if he is, he must learn Spanish or be a wet blanket forever.

You will often meet, in persons of wealth and distinction, an easy degenerate accent in Spanish, strangely at variance with their elegance and culture. These are Creoles of the Antilles, and they form one of the most valued and popular elements of society in the capital. There is a gallantry and dash about the men, and an intelligence and independence about the women, that distinguish them from their cousins of the Peninsula. The American element has recently grown very prominent in the political and social world. Admiral Topete is a Mexican. His wife is one of the distinguished Cuban family of Arrieta. General Prim married a Mexican heiress. The magnificent Duchess de la Torre, wife of the Regent Serrano, is a Cuban born and bred.

In one particular Madrid is unique among capitals,—it has no suburbs. It lies in a desolate table-land in the windy waste of New Castile; on the north the snowy Guadarrama chills its breezes, and on every other side the tawny landscape stretches away in dwarfish hills and shallow ravines barren of shrub or tree, until distance fuses the vast steppes into one drab plain, which melts in the hazy verge of the warm horizon. There are no villages sprinkled in the environs to lure the Madrilenos out of their walls for a holiday. Those delicious picnics that break with such enchanting freshness and variety the steady course of life in other capitals cannot here exist. No Parisian loves *la bonne ville* so much that he does not call those the happiest of days on which he deserts her for a row at Asnieres, a donkey-ride at Enghien, or a bird-like dinner in the vast chestnuts of Sceaux. "There is only one Kaiserstadt," sings the loyal Kerl of Vienna, but he shakes the dust of the Graben from his feet on holiday mornings, and makes his merry pilgrimage to the lordly Schoen-brunn or the heartsome Dornbach, or the wooded eyry of the Kahlenberg. What would white-bait be if not eaten at Greenwich? What would life be in the great cities without the knowledge that just outside, an hour away from the toil and dust and struggle of this money-getting world, there are green fields, and whispering forests, and verdurous nooks of breezy shadow by the side of brooks where the white pebbles shine through the mottled stream,—where you find great pied pan-sies under your hands, and catch the black beady eyes of orioles watching you from the thickets, and through the lush leafage over you see patches of sky flecked with thin clouds that sail so lazily you cannot be sure if the blue or the white is moving? Existence without these luxuries would be very much like life in Madrid.

Yet it is not so dismal as it might seem. The Grande Duchesse of Gerolstein, the cheeriest moralist who ever occupied a throne, announces just before the curtain falls, "Quand on n'a pas ce qu'on aime, il faut aimer ce qu'on a." But how much easier it is to love what you have when you never imagined anything better! The bulk of the good people of Madrid have never left their natal city. If they have been, for their sins, some day to Val-lecas or Carabanchel or any other of the dusty villages that bake and shiver on the arid plains around them, they give fervid thanks on returning alive, and never wish to go again. They shudder when they hear of the summer excursions of other populations, and commiserate them profoundly for living in a place they are so anxious to leave. A lovely girl of Madrid once said to me she never wished to travel,—some people who had been to France preferred Paris to Madrid; as if that were an inexplicable insanity by which their wanderings had been punished. The indolent incuriousness of the Spaniard accepts the utter isolation of his city as rather an advantage. It saves him the trouble of making up his mind where to go. *Vamonos al Prado!* or, as Browning says, —

"Let's to the Prado and make the most of time."

The people of Madrid take more solid comfort in their promenade than any I know. This is one of the inestimable benefits conferred upon them by those wise and liberal free-thinkers Charles III. and Aranda. They knew how important to the moral and physical health of the people a place of recreation was. They reduced the hideous waste land on the east side of the city to a breathing-space for future generations, turning the meadow into a promenade and the hill into the Buen Retiro. The people growled terribly at the time, as they did at nearly everything this prematurely liberal government did for them. The wise king once wittily said: "My people are like bad children that kick the shins of their nurse whenever their faces are washed."

But they soon became reconciled to their Prado, — a name, by the way, which runs through several idioms, — in Paris they had a Pre-aux-clercs, the Clerks' Meadow, and the great park of Vienna is called the Prater. It was originally the favorite scene of duels, and the cherished trysting-place of lovers. But in modern times it is too popular for any such selfish use.

The polite world takes its stately promenade in the winter afternoons in the northern prolongation of the real Prado, called in the official courtier style *Las delicias de Isabel Segunda,* but in common speech the Castilian Fountain, or *Castellana,* to save time. So perfect is the social discipline in these old countries that people who are not in society never walk in this long promenade, which is open to all the world. You shall see there, any pleasant day before the Carnival, the aristocracy of the kingdom, the fast young hopes of the nobility, the diplomatic body resident, and the flexible figures and graceful bearing of the high-born ladies of Castile. Here they take the air as free from snobbish competition as the good society of Olympus, while a hundred paces farther south, just beyond the Mint, the world at large takes its plebeian constitutional. How long, with a democratic system of government, this purely conventional respect will be paid to blue-ness of blood cannot be conjectured. Its existence a year after the Revolution was to me one of the most singular of phenomena.

After Easter Monday the Castellana is left to its own devices for the summer. With the warm long days of May and June, the evening walk in the Salon begins. Europe affords no scene more original and characteristic. The whole city meets in this starlit drawing-room. It is a vast evening party al fresco, stretching from the Alcala to the Course of San Geronimo. In the wide street beside it every one in town who owns a carriage may be seen moving lazily up and down, and apparently envying the gossiping strollers on foot. On three nights in the week there is music in the Retiro Garden,—not as in our feverish way beginning so early that you must sacrifice your dinner to get there, and then turning you out disconsolate in that seductive hour which John Phoenix used to call the "shank of the evening," but opening sensibly at half past nine and going leisurely forward until after midnight. The music is very good. Sometimes Arban comes down from Paris to recover from his winter fatigues and bewitch the Spains with his wizard *baton*.

In all this vast crowd nobody is in a hurry. They have all night before them. They stayed quietly at home in the stress of the noontide when the sunbeams were falling in the glowing streets like javelins,—they utilized some of the waste hours of the broiling afternoon in sleep, and are fresh as daisies now. The women are not haunted by the thought of lords and babies growling and wailing at home. Their lords are beside them, the babies are sprawling in the clean gravel by their chairs. Late in the small hours I have seen these family parties in the promenade, the husband tranquilly smoking his hundredth cigarette, his *placens uxor* dozing in her chair, one baby asleep on the ground, and another slumbering in her lap.

This Madrid climate is a gallant one, and kindlier to the women than the men. The ladies are built on the old-fashioned generous plan. Like a Southern table in the old times, the only fault is too abundant plenty. They move along with a superb dignity of carriage that Banting would like to banish from the world, their round white shoulders shining in the starlight, their fine heads elegantly draped in the coquettish and always graceful mantilla. But you would look in vain among the men of Madrid for such fulness and liberality of structure. They are thin, eager, sinewy in ap' pearance, — though it is the spareness of the Turk, not of the American. It comes from tobacco and the Guadarrama winds. This still, fine, subtle air that blows from the craggy peaks over the treeless plateau seems to take all superfluous moisture out of the men of Madrid. But it is, like Benedick's wit, "a most manly air, it will not hurt a woman." This tropic summer-time brings the halcyon days of the vagabonds of Madrid. They are a temperate, reasonable people, after all, when they are let alone. They do not require the savage stimulants of our colder-blooded race. The fresh air is a feast. As Walt Whitman says, they loaf and invite their souls. They provide for the banquet only the most spiritual provender. Their dissipation is confined principally to starlight and zephyrs; the coarser and wealthier spirits indulge in ice, agraz, and meringues dissolved in water. The climax of their luxury is a cool bed. Walking about the city at midnight, I have seen the fountains all surrounded by luxurious vagabonds asleep or in revery, dozens of them stretched along the rim of the basins, in the spray of the splashing water, where the least start would plunge them in. But the dreams of these Latin beggars are too peaceful to trouble their slumber. They lie motionless, amid the roar of wheels and the tramp of a thousand feet, their bed the sculptured marble, their covering the deep, amethystine vault, warm and cherishing with its breath of summer winds, bright with its trooping stars. The Providence of the worthless watches and guards them!

The chief commerce of the streets of Madrid seems to be fire and water, bane and antidote. It would be impossible for so many match-venders to live anywhere else, in a city ten times the size of Madrid. On every block you will find a wandering merchant dolefully announcing paper and phosphorus, — the one to construct cigarettes and the other to light them. The matches are little waxen tapers very neatly made and enclosed in pasteboard boxes, which are sold for a cent and contain about a hundred *fosforos*. These boxes are ornamented with portraits of the popular favorites of the day, and afford a very fair test of the progress and decline of parties. The queen has disappeared from them except in caricature, and the chivalrous face of Castelar and the heavy Bourbon mouth of Don Carlos are oftener seen than any others. A Madrid smoker of average industry will use a box a day. They smoke more cigarettes than cigars, and in the ardor of conversation allow their fire to go out every minute. A young Austrian, who was watching a *senorito* light his wisp of paper for the fifth time, and mentally comparing it with the volcano volume and *kern-deutsch* integrity of purpose of the meerschaums of his native land, said to me: "What can you expect of a people who trifle in that way with the only work of their lives?"

It is this habit of constant smoking that makes the Madrilenos the thirstiest people in the world; so that, alternating with the cry of "Fire, lord-lings! Matches, chevaliers!" you hear continually the drone so tempting to parched throats, "Water! who wants water? freezing water! colder than snow!" This is the daily song of the Gallician who marches along in his irrigating mission, with his brown blouse, his short breeches, and pointed hat, like that Aladdin wears in the cheap editions; a little varied by the Valentian in his party-colored mantle and his tow trousers, showing the bronzed leg from the knee to the blue-bordered sandals. Numerous as they are, they all seem to have enough to do. They carry their scriptural-looking water-jars on their backs, and a smart tray of tin and burnished brass, with meringues and glasses, in front. The glasses are of enormous but not extravagant proportions. These dropsical Iberians will drink water as if it were no stronger than beer. In the winter-time, while the cheerful invitation rings out to the same effect, — that the beverage is cold as the snow, — the merchant prudently carries a little pot of hot water over a spirit-lamp to take the chill off for shivery customers.

Madrid is one of those cities where strangers fear the climate less than residents. Nothing is too bad for the Castilian to say of his native air. Before you have been a day in the city some kind soul will warn you against everything you have been in the habit of doing as leading to sudden and severe death in this subtle air. You will hear in a dozen different tones the favorite proverb, which may be translated, —

The air of Madrid is as sharp as a knife, —
It will spare a candle and blow out your life: —

and another where the truth, as in many Spanish proverbs, is sacrificed to the rhyme, saying that the climate is _tres meses invierno y nueve infierno, — _three months winter and nine months Tophet. At the first coming of the winter frosts the genuine son of Madrid gets out his capa, the national full round cloak, and never leaves it off till late in the hot spring days. They have a way of throwing one corner over the left shoulder, so that a bright strip of gay lining falls outward and pleasantly relieves the sombre monotony of the streets. In this way the face is completely covered by the heavy woollen folds, only the eyes being visible under the sombrero. The true Spaniard breathes no out-of-doors air all winter except through his cloak, and they stare at strangers who go about with uncovered faces enjoying the brisk air as if they were lunatics. But what makes the custom absurdly incongruous is that the women have no such terror of fresh air. While the hidalgo goes smothered in his wrappings his wife and daughter wear nothing on their necks and faces but their pretty complexions, and the gallant breeze, grateful for this generous confidence, repays them in roses. I have sometimes fancied that in this land of traditions this difference might have arisen in those days of adventure when the cavaliers had good reasons for keeping their faces concealed, while the senoras, we are bound to believe, have never done anything for which their own beauty was not the best excuse.

Nearly all there is of interest in Madrid consists in the faces and the life of its people. There is but one portion of the city which appeals to the tourist's ordinary set of emotions. This is the old Moors' quarter, — the intricate jumble of streets and places on the western edge of the town, overlooking the bankrupt river. Here is St. Andrew's, the parish church where Isabella the Catholic and her pious husband used to offer their stiff and dutiful prayers. Behind it a market-place of the most primitive kind runs precipitately down to the Street of. Segovia, at such an angle that you wonder the turnips and carrots can ever be brought to keep their places on the rocky slope. If you will wander through the dark alleys and hilly streets of this quarter when twilight is softening the tall tenement-houses to a softer purpose, and the doorways are all full of gossiping groups, and here and there in the little courts you can hear the tinkling of a guitar and the drone of ballads, and see the idlers lounging by the fountains, and everywhere against the purple sky the crosses of old convents, while the evening air is musical with slow chimes from the full-arched belfries, it will not be hard to imagine you are in the Spain you have read and dreamed of. And, climbing out of this labyrinth of slums, you pass under the gloomy gates that lead to the Plaza Mayor. This once magnificent square is now as squalid and forsaken as the Place Royale of Paris, though it dates from a period comparatively recent. The mind so instinctively revolts at the contemplation of those orgies of priestly brutality which have made the very name of this place redolent with a fragrance of scorched Christians, that we naturally assign it an immemorial antiquity. But a glance at the booby face of Philip III. on his round-bellied charger in the centre of the square will remind us that this place was built at the same time the Mayflower's passengers were laying the massive foundations of the great Republic. The Autos-da-Fe, the plays of Lope de Vega, and the bull-fights went on for many years with impartial frequency under the approving eyes of royalty, which occupied a convenient balcony in the Panaderia, that overdressed building with the two extinguisher towers. Down to a period disgracefully near us, those balconies were occupied by the dull-eyed, pendulous-lipped tyrants who have sat on the throne of St. Ferdinand, while there in the spacious court below the varied sports went on, — to-day a comedy of Master Lope, to-morrow the gentle and joyous slaying of bulls, and the next day, with greater pomp and ceremony, with banners hung from the windows, and my lord the king surrounded by his women and his courtiers in their bravest gear, and the august presence of the chief priests and their idol in the form of wine and wafers, — the judg-ment and fiery sentence of the thinking men of Spain.

Let us remember as we leave this accursed spot that the old palace of the Inquisition is now the Ministry of Justice, where a liberal statesman has just drawn up the bill of civil marriage; and that in the convent of the Trinitarians a Spanish Rationalist, the Minister of Fomento, is laboring to secularize education in the Peninsula. There is much coiling and hissing, but the fangs of the ser-pent are much less prompt and effective than of old.

The wide Calle Mayor brings you in a moment out of these mouldy shadows and into the broad light of nowadays which shines in the Puerta del Sol. Here, under the walls of the Ministry of the Interior, the quick, restless heart of Madrid beats with the new life it has lately earned. The flags of the pavement have been often stained with blood, but of blood shed in combat, in the assertion of individual freedom. Although the government holds that fortress-palace with a grasp of iron, it can exercise no control over the free speech that asserts itself on the very sidewalk of the Principal. At every step you see news-stands filled with the sharp critical journalism of Spain, — often ignorant and unjust, but generally courteous in expression and independent in thought. Every day at noon the northern mails bring hither the word of all Europe to the awaking Spanish mind, and within that massive building the converging lines of the telegraph are whispering every hour their persuasive lessons of the world's essential unity.

The movement of life and growth is bearing the population gradually away from that dark mediaeval Madrid of the Catholic kings through the Puerta del Sol to the airy heights beyond, and the new, fresh quarter built by the philosopher Bourbon Charles III. is becoming the most important part of the city. I think we may be permitted to hope that the long reign of savage faith and repression is broken at last, and that this abused and suffering people is about to enter into its rightful inheritance of modern freedom and progress.

SPANISH LIVING AND DYING

Nowhere is the sentiment of home stronger than in Spain. Strangers, whose ideas of the Spanish character have been gained from romance and comedy, are apt to note with some surprise the strength and prevalence of the domestic affections. But a moment's reflection shows us that nothing is more natural. It is the result of all their history. The old Celtic population had scarcely any religion but that of the family. The Goths brought in the pure Teutonic regard for woman and marriage. The Moors were distinguished by the patriarchal structure of their society. The Spaniards have thus learned the lesson of home in the school of history and tradition. The intense feeling of individuality, which so strongly marks the Spanish character, and which in the political world is so fatal an element of strife and obstruction, favors this peculiar domesticity. The Castilian is submissive to his king and his priest, haughty and inflexible with his equals. But his own house is a refuge from the contests of out of doors. The reflex of absolute authority is here observed, it is true. The Spanish father is absolute king and lord by his own hearthstone, but his sway is so mild and so readily acquiesced in that it is hardly felt. The evils of tyranny are rarely seen but by him who resists it, and the Spanish family seldom calls for the harsh exercise of parental authority.

This is the rule. I do not mean to say there are no exceptions. The pride and jealousy inherent in the race make family quarrels, when they do arise, the bitterest and the fiercest in the world. In every grade of life these vindictive feuds among kindred are seen from time to time. Twice at least the steps of the throne have been splashed with royal blood shed by a princely hand. Duels between noble cousins and stabbing affrays between peasant brothers alike attest the unbending sense of personal dignity that still infects this people.

A light word between husbands and wives sometimes goes unexplained, and the rift between them widens through life. I know some houses where the wife enters at one door and the husband at another; where if they meet on the stairs, they do not salute each other. Under the same roof they have lived for years and have not spoken. One word would heal all discord, and that word will never be spoken by either. They cannot be divorced,—the Church is inexorable. They will not incur the scandal of a public separation. So they pass lives of lonely isolation in adjoining apartments, both thinking rather better of each other and of themselves for this devilish persistence.

An infraction of parental discipline is never forgiven. I knew a general whose daughter fell in love with his adjutant, a clever and amiable young officer. He had positively no objection to the suitor, but was surprised that there should be any love-making in his house without his previous suggestion. He refused his consent, and the young people were married without it. The father and son-in-law went off on a campaign, fought, and were wounded in the same battle. The general was asked to recommend his son-in-law for promotion. "I have no son-in-law!" "I mean your daughter's husband." "I have no daughter." "I refer to Lieutenant Don Fulano de Tal. He is a good officer. He distinguished himself greatly in the recent affair." "Ah! otra cosa!" said the grim father-in-law. His hate could not overcome his sense of justice. The youth got his promotion, but his general will not recognize him at the club. It is in the middle and lower classes that the most perfect pictures of the true Spanish family are to be found. The aristocracy is more or less infected with the contagion of Continental manners and morals. You will find there the usual proportion of wives who despise their husbands, and men who neglect their wives, and children who do not honor their parents. The smartness of American "pickles" has even made its appearance among the little countesses of Madrid. A lady was eating an ice one day, hungrily watched by the wide eyes of the infant heiress of the house. As the latter saw the last hope vanishing before the destroying spoon, she cried out, "Thou eatest all and givest me none,—maldita sea tu alma!" (accursed be thy soul). This dreadful imprecation was greeted with roars of laughter from admiring friends, and the profane little innocent was smothered in kisses and cream.

Passing at noon by any of the squares or shady places of Madrid, you will see dozens of laboring-people at their meals. They sit on the ground, around the steaming and savory *cocido* that forms the peasant Spaniard's unvaried dinner. The foundation is of *garbanzos*, the large chick-pea of the country, brought originally to Europe by the Carthaginians,—the Roman *cicer,* which gave its name to the greatest of the Latin orators. All other available vegetables are thrown in; on days of high gala a piece of meat is added, and some forehanded housewives attain the climax of luxury by flavoring the compound with a link of sausage. The mother brings the dinner and her tawny brood of nestlings. A shady spot is selected for the feast. The father dips his wooden spoon first into the vapory bowl, and mother and babes follow with grave decorum. Idle loungers passing these patriarchal groups, on their way to a vapid French breakfast at a restaurant, catch the fragrance of the *olla* and the chatter of the family, and envy the dinner of herbs with love.

There is no people so frugal. We often wonder how a Washington clerk can live on twelve hundred dollars, but this would be luxury in expensive Madrid. It is one of the dearest capitals in Europe. Foreigners are never weary decrying its high prices for poor fare; but Castilians live in good houses, dress well, receive their intimate friends, and hold their own with the best in the promenade, upon incomes that would seem penury to any country parson in America. There are few of the nobility who retain the great fortunes of former days. You can almost tell on your fingers the tale of the grandees in Madrid who can live without counting the cost. The army and navy are crowded with general officers whose political services have obliged their promotion. The state is too much impoverished to pay liberal salaries, and yet the rank of these officers requires the maintenance of a certain social position. Few of them are men of fortune. The result is that necessity has taught them to live well upon little, I knew widows who went everywhere in society, whose daughters were always charmingly dressed, who lived in a decent quarter of the town, and who had no resources whatever but a husband's pension.

The best proof of the capacity of Spaniards to spread a little gold over as much space as a goldbeater could is the enormous competition for pub-lic employment. Half the young men in Spain are candidates for places under government ranging from $250 to $1000. Places of $1500 to $2000 are considered objects of legitimate ambition even to deputies and leading politicians. Expressed in reals these sums have a large and satisfying sound. Fifty dollars seems little enough for a month's work, but a thousand reals has the look of a most respectable salary. In Portugal, however, you can have all the delightful sensations of prodigality at a contemptible cost. You can pay, without serious damage to your purse, five thousand reis for your breakfast.

It is the smallness of incomes and the necessity of looking sharply to the means of life that makes the young people of Madrid so prudent in their love affairs. I know of no place where ugly heir-esses are such belles, and where young men with handsome incomes are so universally esteemed by all who know them. The stars on the sleeves of young officers are more regarded than their dancing, and the red belt of a field officer is as winning in the eyes of beauty as a cestus of Venus. A. subaltern offered his hand and heart to a black-eyed girl of Castile. She said kindly but firmly that the night was too cloudy. "What," said the stupefied lover, "the sky is full of stars." "I see but one," said the prudent beauty, her fine eyes resting pensively upon his cuff, where one lone luminary indicated his rank.

This spirit is really one of forethought, and not avarice. People who have enough for two almost always marry from inclination, and frequently take partners for life without a penny.

If men were never henpecked except by learned wives, Spain would be the place of all others for timid men to marry in. The girls are bright, vivacious, and naturally very clever, but they have scarcely any education whatever. They never know the difference between *b* and *v*. They throw themselves in orthography entirely upon your benevolence. They know a little music and a little French, but they have never crossed, even in a school-day excursion, the border line of the ologies. They do not even read novels. They are regarded as injurious, and cannot be trusted to the daughters until mamma has read them. Mamma never has time to read them, and so they are condemned by default. Fernan Caballero, in one of her sleepy little romances, refers to this illiterate character of the Spanish ladies, and says it is their chief charm, — that a Christian woman, in good society, ought not to know anything beyond her cookery-book and her missal. There is-an old proverb which coarsely conveys this idea: A mule that whinnies and a woman that talks Latin never come to any good.

There is a contented acquiescence in this moral servitude among the fair Spaniards which would madden our agitatresses. (See what will become of the language when male words are crowded out of the dictionary!)

It must be the innocence which springs from ignorance that induces an occasional coarseness of expression which surprises you in the conversation of those lovely young girls. They will speak with perfect freedom of the *etat-civil* of a young unmarried mother. A maiden of fifteen said to me: "I must go to a party this evening *decolletee,* and I hate it. Benigno is getting old enough to marry, and he wants to see all the girls in low neck before he makes up his mind." They all swear like troopers, without a thought of profanity. Their mildest expression of surprise is Jesus Maria! They change their oaths with the season. At the feast of the Immaculate Conception, the favorite oath is Maria Purissima. This is a time of especial interest to young girls. It is a period of compulsory confession, — conscience-cleaning, as they call it. They are all very pious in their way. They attend to their religious duties with the same interest which they displayed a few years before in dressing and undressing their dolls, and will display a few years later in putting the lessons they learned with their dolls to a more practical use.

The visible concrete symbols and observances of religion have great influence with them. They are fond of making vows in tight places and faithfully observing them afterwards. In an hour's walk in the streets of Madrid you will see a dozen ladies with a leather strap buckled about their slender waists and hanging nearly to the ground. Others wear a knotted cord and tassels. These are worn as the fulfilment of vows, or penances.

I am afraid they give rise to much worldly conjecture on the part of idle youth as to what amiable sins these pretty penitents can have been guilty of. It is not prudent to ask an explanation of the peculiar mercy, or remorse, which this purgatorial strap commemorates.

You will probably not enlarge your stock of knowledge further than to learn that the lady in question considers you a great nuisance.

The graceful lady who, in ascending the throne of France, has not ceased to be a thorough Spaniard, still preserves these pretty weaknesses of her youth. She vowed a chapel to her patron saint if her firstborn was a man-child, and paid it. She has hung a vestal lamp in the Church of Notre Dame des Victoires, in pursuance of a vow she keeps rigidly secret. She is a firm believer in relics also, and keeps a choice assortment on hand in the Tuileries for sudden emergencies. When old Baciocchi lay near his death, worn out by a horrible nervous disorder which would not let him sleep, the empress told the doctors, with great mystery, that she would cure him. After a few preliminary masses, she came into his room and hung on his bedpost a little gold-embroidered sachet containing (if the evidence of holy men is to be believed) a few threads of the swaddling-clothes of John the Baptist. Her simple childlike faith wrung the last grim smile from the tortured lips of the dying courtier.

The very names of the Spanish women are a constant reminder of their worship. They are all named out of the calendar of saints and virgin martyrs. A large majority are christened Mary; but as this sacred name by much use has lost all distinctive meaning, some attribute, some especial invocation of the Virgin, is always coupled with it. The names of Dolores, Mercedes, Milagros, recall Our Lady of the Sorrows, of the Gifts, of the Miracles. I knew a hoydenish little gypsy who bore the tearful name of Lagrimas. The most appropriate name I heard for these large-eyed, soft-voiced beauties was Peligros, Our Lady of Dangers. Who could resist the comforting assurance of "Consuelo"? "Blessed," says my Lord Lytton, "is woman who consoles." What an image of maiden purity goes with the name of Nieves, the Virgin of the Snows! From a single cotillon of Castilian girls you can construct the whole history of Our Lady; Conception, Annunciation, Sorrows, Solitude, Assumption. As young ladies are never called by their family names, but always by their baptismal appellations, you cannot pass an evening in a Spanish *tertulia* without being reminded of every stage in the life of the Immaculate Mother, from Bethlehem to Calvary and beyond.

The common use of sacred words is universal in Catholic countries, but nowhere so striking as in Spain. There is a little solemnity in the French adieu. But the Spaniard says adios instead of "good-morning." No letter closes without the prayer, "God guard your Grace many years!" They say a judge announces to a murderer his sentence of death with the sacramental wish of length of days. There is something a little shocking to a Yankee mind in the label of Lachryma Christi; but in La Mancha they call fritters the Grace of God.

The piety of the Spanish women does not prevent them from seeing some things clearly enough with their bright eyes. One of the most bigoted women in Spain recently said: "I hesitate to let my child go to confession. The priests ask young girls such infamous questions, that my cheeks burn when I think of them, after all these years." I stood one Christmas Eve in the cold midnight wind, waiting for the church doors to open for the night mass, the famous *misa del gallo*. On the steps beside me sat a decent old woman with her two daughters. At last she rose and said, "Girls, it is no use waiting any longer. The priests won't leave their housekeepers this cold night to save anybody's soul." In these two cases, taken from the two extremes of the Catholic society, there was no disrespect for the Church or for religion. Both these women believed with a blind faith. But they could not help seeing how unclean were the hands that dispensed the bread of life.

The respect shown to the priesthood as a body is marvellous, in view of the profligate lives of many. The general progress of the age has forced most of the dissolute priests into hypocrisy. But their cynical immorality is still the bane of many families. And it needs but a glance at the vile manual of confession, called the Golden Key, the author of which is the too well known Padre Claret, confessor to the queen, to see the systematic moral poisoning the minds of Spanish women must undergo who pay due attention to what is called their religious duties. If a confessor obeys the injunctions of this high ecclesiastical authority, his fair penitents will have nothing to learn from a diligent perusal of Faublas or Casanova. It would, however, be unjust to the priesthood to consider them all as corrupt as royal chaplains. It requires a combination of convent and palace life to produce these finished specimens of mitred infamy.

It is to be regretted that the Spanish women are kept in such systematic ignorance. They have a quicker and more active intelligence than the men. With a fair degree of education, much might be hoped from them in the intellectual development of the country. In society, you will at once be struck with the superiority of the women to their husbands and brothers in cleverness and appreciation. Among small tradesmen, the wife always comes to the rescue of her slow spouse when she sees him befogged in a bargain. In the fields, you ask a peasant some question about your journey. He will hesitate, and stammer, and end with, *"Quien sabe?"* but his wife will answer with glib completeness all you want to know. I can imagine no cause for this, unless it be that the men cloud their brains all day with the fumes of tobacco, and the women do not.

The personality of the woman is not so entirely merged in that of the husband as among us. She retains her own baptismal and family name through life. If Miss Matilda Smith marries Mr. Jonathan Jones, all vestige of the former gentle being vanishes at once from the earth, and Mrs. Jonathan Jones alone remains. But in Spain she would become Mrs. Matilda Smith de Jones, and her eldest-born would be called Don Juan Jones y Smith. You ask the name of a married lady in society, and you hear as often her own name as that of her husband.

Even among titled people, the family name seems more highly valued than the titular designation. Everybody knows Narvaez, but how few have heard of the Duke of Valencia! The Regent Serrano has a name known and honored over the world, but most people must think twice before they remember the Duke de la Torre. Juan Prim is better known than the Marques de los Castillejos ever will be. It is perhaps due to the prodigality with which titles have been scattered in late years that the older titles are more regarded than the new, although of inferior grade. Thus Prim calls himself almost invariably the Conde de Reus, though his grandeeship came with his investiture as marquis.

There is something quite noticeable about this easy way of treating one's name. We are accustomed to think a man can have but one name, and can sign it but in one way. Lord Derby can no more call himself Mr. Stanley than President Grant can sign a bill as U. Simpson. Yet both these signatures would be perfectly valid according to Spanish analogy. The Marquis of Santa Marta signs himself Guzman; the Marquis of Albaida uses no signature but Orense; both of these gentlemen being Republican deputies. I have seen General Prim's name signed officially, Conde de Reus, Marques de los Castillejos, Prim, J. Prim, Juan Prim, and Jean Prim, changing the style as often as the humor strikes him.

Their forms of courtesy are, however, invariable. You can never visit a Spaniard without his informing you that you are in your own house. If, walking with him, you pass his residence, he asks you to enter your house and unfatigue yourself a moment. If you happen upon any Spaniard, of whatever class, at the hour of repast, he always offers you his dinner; if you decline, it must be with polite wishes for his digestion. With the Spaniards, no news is good news; it is therefore civil to ask a Spaniard if his lady-wife goes on without novelty, and to express your profound gratification on being assured that she does. Their forms of hospitality are evidently Moorish, derived from the genuine open hand and open tent of the children of the desert; now nothing is left of them but grave and decorous words. In the old times, one who would have refused such offers would have been held a churl; now one who would accept them would be regarded as a boor.

There is still something primitive about the Spanish servants. A flavor of the old romances and the old comedy still hangs about them. They are chatty and confidential to a degree that appalls a stiff and formal Englishman of the upper middle class. The British servant is a chilly and statuesque image of propriety. The French is an intelligent and sympathizing friend. You can make of him what you like. But the Italian, and still more the Spaniard, is as gay as a child, and as incapable of intentional disrespect. The Castilian grandee does not regard his dignity as in danger from a moment's chat with a waiter. He has no conception of that ferocious decorum we Anglo-Saxons require from our manservants and our maidservants. The Spanish servant seems to regard it as part of his duty to keep your spirits gently excited while you dine by the gossip of the day. He joins also in your discussions, whether they touch lightly on the politics of the hour or plunge profoundly into the depths of philosophic research. He laughs at your wit, and swings his napkin with convulsions of mirth at your good stories. He tells you the history of his life while you are breaking your egg, and lays the story of his loves before you with your coffee. Yet he is not intrusive. He will chatter on without waiting for a reply, and when you are tired of him you can shut him off with a word. There are few Spanish servants so uninteresting but that you can find in them from time to time some sparks of that ineffable light which shines forever in Sancho and Figaro.

The traditions of subordination, which are the result of long centuries of tyranny, have prevented the development of that feeling of independence among the lower orders, which in a freer race finds its expression in ill manners and discourtesy to superiors. I knew a gentleman in the West whose circumstances had forced him to become a waiter in a backwoods restaurant. He bore a deadly grudge at the profession that kept him from starving, and asserted his unconquered nobility of soul by scowling at his customers and swearing at the viands he dispensed. I remember the deep sense of wrong with which he would growl, "Two buckwheats, begawd!" You see nothing of this defiant spirit in Spanish servants. They are heartily glad to find employment, and ask no higher good-fortune than to serve acceptably. As to drawing comparisons between themselves and their masters, they never seem to think they belong to the same race. I saw a pretty grisette once stop to look at a show-window where there was a lay-figure completely covered with all manner of trusses. She gazed at it long and earnestly, evidently thinking it was some new fashion just introduced into the gay world. At last she tripped away with all the grace of her unfettered limbs, saying, "If the fine ladies have to wear all those machines, I am glad I am not made like them."

Whether it be from their more regular and active lives, or from their being unable to pay for medical attendance, the poorer classes suffer less from sickness than their betters. An ordinary Spaniard is sick but once in his life, and that once is enough,—'twill serve. The traditions of the old satires which represented the doctor and death as always hunting in couples still survive in Spain. It is taken as so entirely a matter of course that a patient must die that the law of the land imposed a heavy fine upon physicians who did not bring a priest on their second visit. His labor of exhortation and confession was rarely wasted. There were few sufferers who recovered from the shock of that solemn ceremony in their chambers. Medical science still labors in Spain under the ban of ostracism, imposed in the days when all research was impiety. The Inquisition clamored for the blood of Vesalius, who had committed the crime of a demonstration in anatomy. He was forced into a pilgrimage of expiation, and died on the way to Palestine. The Church has always looked with a jealous eye upon the inquirers, the innovators. Why these probes, these lancets, these multifarious drugs, when the object in view could be so much more easily obtained by the judicious application of masses and prayers?

So it has come about that the doctor is a Pariah, and miracles flourish in the Peninsula. At every considerable shrine you will see the walls covered with waxen models of feet, legs, hands, and arms secured by the miraculous interposition of the *genius loci,* and scores of little crutches attesting the marvellous hour when they became useless. Each shrine, like a mineral spring, has its own especial virtue. A Santiago medal was better than quinine for ague. St. Veronica's handkerchief is sovereign for sore eyes. A bone of St. Magin supersedes the use of mercury. A finger-nail of San Frutos cured at Segovia a case of congenital idiocy. The Virgin of Ona acted as a vermifuge on royal infantas, and her girdle at Tortosa smooths their passage into this world. In this age of unfaith relics have lost much of their power. They turn out their score or so of miracles every feast-day, it is true, but are no longer capable of the *tours de force* of earlier days. Cardinal de Retz saw with his eyes a man whose wooden legs were turned to capering flesh and blood by the image of the Pillar of Saragossa. But this was in the good old times before newspapers and telegraphs had come to dispel the twilight of belief.

Now, it is excessively probable that neither doctor nor priest can do much if the patient is hit in earnest. He soon succumbs, and is laid out in his best clothes in an improvised chapel and duly sped on his way. The custom of burying the dead in the gown and cowl of monks has greatly passed into disuse. The mortal relics are treated with growing contempt, as the superstitions of the people gradually lose their concrete character. The soul is the important matter which the Church now looks to. So the cold clay is carted off to the cemetery with small ceremony. Even the coffins of the rich are jammed away into receptacles too small for them, and hastily plastered out of sight. The poor are carried off on trestles and huddled into their nameless graves, without following or blessing. Children are buried with some regard to the old Oriental customs. The coffin is of some gay and cheerful color, pink or blue, and is carried open to the grave by four of the dead child's young companions, a fifth walking behind with the ribboned coffin-lid. I have often seen these touching little parties moving through the bustling streets, the peaceful small face asleep under the open sky, decked with the fading roses and withering lilies. In all well-to-do families the house of death is deserted immediately after the funeral. The stricken ones retire to some other habitation, and there pass eight days in strict and inviolable seclusion. On the ninth day the great masses for the repose of the soul of the departed are said in the parish church, and all the friends of the family are expected to be present. These masses are the most important and expensive incident of the funeral. They cost from two hundred to one thousand dollars, according to the strength and fervor of the orisons employed. They are repeated several years on the anniversary of the decease, and afford a most sure and nourishing revenue to the Church. They are founded upon those feelings inseparable from every human heart, vanity and affection. Our dead friends must be as well prayed for as those of others, and who knows but that they may be in deadly need of prayers! To shorten their fiery penance by one hour, who would not fast for a week? On these anniversaries a black-bordered advertisement appears in the newspapers, headed by the sign of the cross and the Requiescat in Pace, announcing that on this day twelve months Don Fulano de Tal passed from earth garnished with the holy sacraments, that all the masses this day celebrated in such and such churches will be applied to the benefit of his spirit's repose, and that all Christian friends are hereby requested to commend his soul this day unto God. These efforts, if they do the dead no good, at least do the living no harm.

A luxury of grief, in those who can afford it, consists in shutting up the house where a death has taken place and never suffering it to be opened again. I once saw a beautiful house and wide garden thus abandoned in one of the most fashionable streets of Madrid. I inquired about it, and found it was formerly the residence of the Duke of ———. His wife had died there many years before, and since that day not a door nor a window had been opened. The garden gates were red and rough with rust. Grass grew tall and rank in the gravelled walks. A thick lush undergrowth had overrun the flower-beds and the lawns. The blinds were rotting over the darkened windows. Luxuriant vines clambered over all the mossy doors. The stucco was peeling from the walls in unwholesome blotches. Wild birds sang all day in the safe solitude. There was something impressive in this spot of mould and silence, lying there so green and implacable in the very heart of a great and noisy city. The duke lived in Paris, leading the rattling life of a man of the world. He never would sell or let that Madrid house. Perhaps in his heart also, that battered thoroughfare worn by the pattering boots of Ma-bine and the Bois, and the Quartier Breda, there was a green spot sacred to memory and silence, where no footfall should ever light, where no living voice should ever be heard, shut out from the world and its cares and its pleasures, where through the gloom of dead days he could catch a glimpse of a white hand, a flash of a dark eye, the rustle of a trailing robe, and feel sweeping over him the old magic of love's young dream, softening his fancy to tender regret and his eyes to a happy mist—

"Like that which kept the heart of Eden green
Before the useful trouble of the rain."

INFLUENCE OF TRADITION IN SPANISH LIFE

Intelligent Spaniards with whom I have conversed on political matters have often exclaimed, "Ah, you Americans are happy! you have no traditions." The phrase was at first a puzzling one. We Americans are apt to think we have traditions,—a rather clearly marked line of precedents. And it is hard to see how a people should be happier without them. It is not anywhere considered a misfortune to have had a grandfather, I believe, and some very good folks take an innocent pride in that very natural fact. It was not easy to conceive why the possession of a glorious history of many centuries should be regarded as a drawback. But a closer observation of Spanish life and thought reveals the curious and hurtful effect of tradition upon every phase of existence.

In the commonest events of every day you will find the flavor of past ages lingering in petty annoyances. The insecurity of the middle ages has left as a legacy to our times a complicated system of obstacles to a man getting into his own house at night. I lived in a pleasant house on the Prado, with a minute garden in front, and an iron gate and railing. This gate was shut and locked by the night watchman of the quarter at midnight,—so conscientiously that he usually had everything snug by half past eleven. As the same man had charge of a dozen or more houses, it was scarcely reasonable to expect him to be always at your own gate when you arrived. But by a singular fatality I think no man ever found him in sight at any hour. He is always opening some other gate or shutting some other door, or settling the affairs of the nation with a friend in the next block, or carrying on a chronic courtship at the lattice of some olive-cheeked soubrette around the corner. Be that as it may, no one ever found him on hand; and there is nothing to do but to sit down on the curbstone and lift up your voice and shriek for him until he comes. At two o'clock of a morning in January the exercise is not improving to the larynx or the temper. There is a tradition in the very name of this worthy. He is called the Sereno, because a century or so ago he used to call the hour and the state of the weather, and as the sky is almost always cloudless here, he got the name of the Sereno, as the quail is called Bob White, from much iteration. The Sereno opens your gate and the door of your house. When you come to your own floor you must ring, and your servant takes a careful survey of you through a latticed peep-hole before he will let you in. You may positively forbid this every day in the year, but the force of habit is too strong in the Spanish mind to suffer amendment.

This absurd custom comes evidently down from a time of great lawlessness and license, when no houses were secure without these precautions, when people rarely stirred from their doors after nightfall, and when a door was never opened to a stranger. Now, when no such dangers exist, the annoying and senseless habit still remains, because no one dreams of changing anything which their fathers thought proper. Three hundred thousand people in Madrid submit year after year to this nightly cross, and I have never heard a voice raised in protest, nor even in defence of the custom.

There is often a bitterness of opposition to evident improvement which is hard to explain. In the last century, when the eminent naturalist Bowles went down to the Almaden silver-mines, by appointment of the government, to see what was the cause of their exhaustion, he found that they had been worked entirely in perpendicular shafts instead of following the direction of the veins. He perfected a plan for working them in this simple and reasonable way, and no earthly power could make the Spanish miners obey his orders. There was no precedent for this new process, and they would not touch it. They preferred starvation rather than offend the memory of their fathers by a change. At last they had to be dismissed and a full force imported from Germany, under whose hands the mines became instantly enormously productive.

I once asked a very intelligent English contractor why he used no wheelbarrows in his work. He had some hundreds of stalwart navvies employed carrying dirt in small wicker baskets to an embankment. He said the men would not use them. Some said it broke their backs. Others discovered a capital way of amusing themselves by putting the barrow on their heads and whirling the wheel as rapidly as possible with their hands. This was a game which never grew stale. The contractor gave up in despair, and went back to the baskets. But it is in the official regions that tradition is most powerful. In the budget of 1870 there was a curious chapter called "Charges of Justice." This consisted of a collection of articles appropriating large sums of money for the payment of feudal taxes to the great aristocracy of the kingdom as a compensation for long extinct seigniories. The Duke of Rivas got thirteen hundred dollars for carrying the mail to Victoria. The Duke of San Carlos draws ten thousand dollars for carrying the royal correspondence to the Indies. Of course this service ceased to belong to these families some centuries ago, but the salary is still paid. The Duke of Almodovar is well paid for supplying the *baton* of office to the Alguazil of Cordova. The Duke of Osuna—one of the greatest grandees of the kingdom, a gentleman who has the right to wear seventeen hats in the presence of the Queen—receives fifty thousand dollars a year for imaginary feudal services. The Count of Altamira, who, as his name indicates, is a gentleman of high views, receives as a salve for the suppression of his fief thirty thousand dollars a year. In consideration of this sum he surrenders, while it is punctually paid, the privilege of hanging his neighbors.

When the budget was discussed, a Republican member gently criticised this chapter; but his amendment for an investigation of these charges was indignantly rejected. He was accused of a shocking want of Espanolismo. He was thought to have no feeling in his heart for the glories of Spain. The respectability of the Chamber could find but one word injurious enough to express their contempt for so shameless a proposition; they said it was little better than socialism. The "charges" were all voted. Spain, tottering on the perilous verge of bankruptcy, her schoolmasters not paid for months, her sinking fund plundered, her credit gone out of sight, borrowing every cent she spends at thirty per cent., is proud of the privilege of paying into the hands of her richest and most useless class this gratuity of twelve million reals simply because they are descended from the robber chiefs of the darker ages. There is a curious little comedy played by the family of Medina Celi at every new coronation of a king of Spain. The duke claims to be the rightful heir to the throne. He is descended from Prince Ferdinand, who, dying before his father, Don Alonso X., left his babies exposed to the cruel kind-ness of their uncle Sancho, who, to save them the troubles of the throne, assumed it himself and transmitted it to his children, — all this some half dozen centuries ago. At every coronation the duke formally protests; an athletic and sinister-looking court headsman comes down to his palace in the Carrera San Geronimo, and by threats of immediate decapitation induces the duke to sign a paper abdicating his rights to the throne of all the Spains. The duke eats the Bourbon leek with inward profanity, and feels that he has done a most clever and proper thing. This performance is apparently his only object and mission in life. This one sacrifice to tradition is what he is born for.

The most important part of a Spaniard's signature is the *rubrica* or flourish with which it closes. The monarch's hand is set to public acts exclusively by this *parafe.* This evidently dates from the time when none but priests could write. In Madrid the mule-teams are driven tandem through the wide streets, because this was necessary in the ages when the streets were narrow.

There is even a show of argument sometimes to justify an adher-ence to things as they are. About a century ago there was an effort made by people who had lived abroad, and so become conscious of the possession of noses, to have the streets of Madrid cleaned. The proposition was at first received with apathetic contempt, but when the innovators persevered they met the earnest and successful op-position of all classes. The Cas-tilian *savans* gravely reported that the air of Madrid, which blew down from the snowy Guadarra-mas, was so thin and piercing that it absolutely needed the gentle correc-tive of the ordure-heaps to make it fit for human lungs.

There is no nation in Europe in which so little washing is done. I do not think it is because the Spaniards do not want to be neat. They are, on the whole, the best-dressed people on the Continent. The hate of ablutions descends from those centuries of warfare with the Moors. The heathens washed themselves daily; therefore a Christian should not. The monks, who were too lazy to bathe, taught their followers to be filthy by precept and example. Water was never to be applied externally except in baptism. It was a treacherous ele-ment, and dallying with it had gotten Bathsheba and Susanna into no end of trouble. So when the cleanly infidels were driven out of Granada, the pious and hydrophobic Cardinal Ximenez persuaded the Catholic sovereigns to destroy the abomination of baths they left behind. Until very recently the Spanish mind has been unable to separate a certain idea of immorality from bathing. When Madame Daunoy, one of the sprightliest of observers, visited the court of Philip IV., she found it was considered shocking among the ladies of the best society to wash the face and hands. Once or twice a week they would glaze their pretty visages with the white of an egg. Of late years this prejudice has given way somewhat; but it has lasted longer than any monument in Spain.

These, however, are but trivial manifestations of that power of tradition which holds the Spanish intellect imprisoned as in a vice of iron. The whole life of the nation is fatally influenced by this blind reverence for things that have been. It may be said that by force of tradition Christian morality has been driven from individual life by religion, and honesty has been supplanted as a rule of public conduct by honor, — a wretched substitute in either case, and irreconcilably at war with the spirit of the age.

The growth of this double fanaticism is easily explained; it is the result of centuries of religious wars. From the hour when Pelayo, the first of the Asturian kings, successfully met and repulsed the hitherto victorious Moors in his rocky fortress of Covadonga, to the day when Boabdil the Unlucky saw for the last time through streaming tears the vermilion towers of Alhambra crowned with the banner of the cross, there was not a year of peace in Spain. No other nation has had such an experience. Seven centuries of constant warfare, with three thousand battles; this is the startling epitome of Spanish history from the Mahometan conquest to the reign of Ferdinand and Isabella. In this vast war there was laid the foundation of the national character of to-day.

Even before the conquering Moslem crossed from Africa, Spain was the most deeply religious country in Europe; and by this I mean the country in which the Church was most powerful in its relations with the State. When the Council of Toledo, in 633, received the king of Castile, he fell on his face at the feet of the bishops before venturing to address them. When the hosts of Islam had overspread the Peninsula, and the last remnant of Christianity had taken refuge in the inaccessible hills of the northwest, the richest possession they carried into these inviolate fastnesses was a chest of relics,— knuckle-bones of apostles and splinters of true crosses, in which they trusted more than in mortal arms. The Church had thus a favorable material to work upon in the years of struggle that followed. The circumstances all lent themselves to the scheme of spiritual domination. The fight was for the cross against the crescent; the symbol of the quarrel was visible and tangible. The Spaniards were poor and ignorant and credulous. The priests were enough superior to lead and guide them, and not so far above them as to be out of the reach of their sympathies and their love. They marched with them. They shared their toils and dangers. They stimulated their hate of the enemy. They taught them that their cruel anger was the holy wrath of God. They held the keys of eternal weal or woe, and rewarded subservience to the priestly power with promises of everlasting felicity; while the least symptom of rebellion in thought or action was punished with swift death and the doom of endless flames. There was nothing in the Church which the fighting Spaniard could recognize as a reproach to himself. It was as bitter, as brave, as fierce, and revengeful as he. His credulity regarded it as divine, and worthy of blind adoration, and his heart went out to it with the sympathy of perfect love.

In these centuries of war there was no commerce, no manufactures, no settled industry of importance among the Spaniards. There was consequently no wealth, none of that comfort and ease which is the natural element of doubt and discussion. Science did not exist. The little learning of the time was exclusively in the hands of the priesthood. If from time to time an intelligent spirit struggled against the chain of unquestioning bigotry that bound him, he was rigorously silenced by prompt and bloody punishment. There seemed to be no need of discussion, no need of inculcation of doctrine. The serious work of the time was the war with the infidel. The clergy managed everything. The question, "What shall I do to be saved?" never entered into those simple and ignorant minds. The Church would take care of those who did her bidding.

Thus it was that in the hammering of those struggling ages the nation became welded together in one compact mass of unquestioning, unreasoning faith, which the Church could manage at its own good pleasure.

It was also in these times that Spanish honor took its rise. This sentiment is so nearly connected with that of personal loyalty that they may be regarded as phases of the same monarchical spirit. The rule of honor as distinguished from honesty and virtue is the most prominent characteristic of monarchy, and for that reason the political theorists from the time of Montesquieu have pronounced in favor of the monarchy as a more practicable form of government than the republic, as requiring a less perfect and delicate machinery, men of honor being far more common than men of virtue. As in Spain, owing to special conditions, monarchy attained the most perfect growth and development which the world has seen, the sentiment of honor, as a rule of personal and political action, has there reached its most exaggerated form. I use this word, of course, in its restricted meaning of an intense sense of personal dignity, and readiness to sacrifice for this all considerations of interest and morality.

This phase of the Spanish character is probably derived in its germ from the Gothic blood of their ancestors. Their intense self-assertion has been, in the Northern races, modified by the progress of intelligence and the restraints of municipal law into a spirit of sturdy self-respect and a disinclination to submit to wrong. The Goths of Spain have unfortunately never gone through this civilizing process. Their endless wars never gave an opportunity for the development of the purely civic virtues of respect and obedience to law. The people at large were too wretched, too harried by constant coming and going of the waves of war, to do more than live, in a shiftless, hand-to-mouth way, from the proceeds of their flocks and herds. There were no cities of importance within the Spanish lines. There was no opportunity for the growth of the true burgher spirit.

There was no law to speak of in all these years except the twin despotism of the Church and the king. If there had been dissidence between them it might have been better for the people. But up to late years there has never been a quarrel between the clergy and the crown. Their interests were so identified that the dual tyranny was stronger than even a single one could have been. The crown always lending to the Church when necessary the arm of flesh, and the Church giving to the despotism of the sceptre the sanction of spiritual authority, an absolute power was established over body and soul.

The spirit of individual independence inseparable from Gothic blood being thus forced out of its natural channels of freedom of thought and municipal liberty, it remained in the cavaliers of the army of Spain in the same barbarous form which it had held in the Northern forests,—a physical self-esteem and a readiness to fight on the slightest provocation. This did not interfere with the designs of the Church and was rather a useful engine against its enemies. The absolute power of the crown kept the spirit of feudal arrogance in check while the pressure of a common danger existed. The close cohesion which was so necessary in camp and Church prevented the tendency to disintegration, while the right of life and death was freely exercised by the great lords on their distant estates without interference. The predominating power of the crown was too great and too absolute to result in the establishment of any fixed principle of obedience to law. The union of crozier and sceptre had been, if anything, too successful. The king was so far above the nobility that there was no virtue in obeying him. His commission was divine, and he was no more confined by human laws than the stars and the comets. The obedience they owed and paid him was not respect to law. It partook of the character of religious worship, and left untouched and untamed in their savage hearts the instinct of resistance to all earthly claims of authority.

Such was the condition of the public spirit of Spain at the beginning of that wonderful series of reigns from Ferdinand and Isabella to their great-grandson Philip II., which in less than a century raised Spain to the summit of greatness and built up a realm on which the sun never set. All the events of these prodigious reigns contributed to increase and intensify the national traits to which we have referred. The discovery of America flooded Europe with gold, and making the better class of Spaniards the richest people in the world naturally heightened their pride and arrogance. The long and eventful religious wars of Charles V. and Philip II. gave employment and distinction to thousands of families whose vanity was nursed by the royal favor, and whose ferocious self-will was fed and pampered by the blood of heretics and the spoil of rebels.

The national qualities of superstition and pride made the whole cavalier class a wieldy and effective weapon in the hands of the monarch, and the use he made of them reacted upon these very traits, intensifying and affirming them.

So terrible was this absolute command of the spiritual and physical forces of the kingdom possessed by the monarchs of that day, that when the Reformation flashed out, a beacon in the northern sky of political and religious freedom to the world, its light could not penetrate into Spain. There was a momentary struggle there, it is true. But so apathetic was the popular mind that the effort to bring it into sympathy with the vast movement of the age was hopeless from the beginning. The axe and the fagot made rapid work of the heresy. After only ten years of burnings and beheadings Philip II. could boast that not a heretic lived in his borders.

Crazed by his success and his unquestioned omnipotence at home, and drunken with the delirious dream that God's wrath was breathing through him upon a revolted world, he essayed to crush heresy throughout Europe; and in this mad and awful crime his people undoubtingly seconded him. In this he failed, the stars in their courses fighting against him, the God that his worship slandered taking sides against him. But history records what rivers of blood he shed in the long and desperate fight, and how lovingly and adoringly his people sustained him. He killed, in cold blood, some forty thousand harmless people for their faith, besides the vastly greater number whose lives he took in battle.

Yet this horrible monster, who is blackened with every crime at which humanity shudders, who had no grace of manhood, no touch of humanity, no gleam of sympathy which could redeem the gloomy picture of his ravening life, was beloved and worshipped as few men have been since the world has stood. The common people mourned him at his death with genuine unpaid sobs and tears. They will weep even yet at the story of his edifying death, — this monkish vampire breathing his last with his eyes fixed on the cross of the mild Nazarene, and tormented with impish doubts as to whether he had drunk blood enough to fit him for the company of the just!

His successors rapidly fooled away the stupendous empire that had filled the sixteenth century with its glory. Spain sank from the position of ruler of the world and queen of the seas to the place of a second-rate power, by reason of the weakening power of superstition and bad government, and because the people and the chieftains had never learned the lesson of law.

The clergy lost no tittle of their power. They went on, gayly roasting their heretics and devouring the substance of the people, more prosperous than ever in those days of national decadence. Philip III. gave up the government entirely to the Duke of Lerma, who formed an alliance with the Church, and they led together a joyous life. In the succeeding reign the Church had become such a gnawing cancer upon the state that the servile Cortes had the pluck to protest against its inroads. There were in 1626 nine thousand monasteries for men, besides nunneries. There were thirty-two thousand Dominican and Franciscan friars. In the diocese of Seville alone there were fourteen thousand chaplains. There was a panic in the land. Every one was rushing to get into holy orders. The Church had all the bread. Men must be monks or starve. *Zelus domus tuae come-dit me,* writes the British ambassador, detailing these facts.

We must remember that this was the age when the vast modern movement of inquiry and investigation was beginning. Bacon was laying in England the foundations of philosophy, casting with his prophetic intelligence the horoscope of unborn sciences. Descartes was opening new vistas of thought to the world. But in Spain, while the greatest names of her literature occur at this time, they aimed at no higher object than to amuse their betters. Cervantes wrote Quixote, but he died in a monk's hood; and Lope de Vega was a familiar of the Inquisition. The sad story of the mind of Spain in this momentous period may be written in one word,—everybody believed and nobody inquired.

The country sank fast into famine and anarchy. The madness of the monks and the folly of the king expelled the Moors in 1609, and the loss of a million of the best mechanics and farmers of Spain struck the nation with a torpor like that of death. In 1650 Sir Edward

Hyde wrote that "affairs were in huge disorder." People murdered each other for a loaf of bread. The marine perished for want of sailors. In the stricken land nothing flourished but the rabble of monks and the royal authority.

This is the curious fact. The Church and the Crown had brought them to this misery, yet better than their lives the Spaniards loved the Church and the Crown. A word against either would have cost any man his life in those days. The old alliance still hung together firmly. The Church bullied and dragooned the king in private, but it valued his despotic power too highly ever to slight it in public. There was something superhuman about the faith and veneration with which the people, and the aristocracy as well, regarded the person of the king. There was somewhat of gloomy and ferocious dignity about Philip II. which might easily bring a courtier to his knees; but how can we account for the equal reverence that was paid to the ninny Philip III., the debauched trifler Philip IV., and the drivelling idiot Charles II.?

Yet all of these were invested with the same attributes of the divine. Their hands, like those of Midas, had the gift of making anything they touched too precious for mortal use. A horse they had mounted could never be ridden again. A woman they had loved must enter a nunnery when they were tired of her.

When Buckingham came down to Spain with Charles of England, the Conde-Duque of Olivares was shocked and scandalized at the relation of confidential friendship that existed between the prince and the duke. The world never saw a prouder man than Olivares. His picture by Velazquez hangs side by side with that of his royal master in Madrid. You see at a glance that the count-duke is the better man physically, mentally, morally. But he never dreamed it. He thought in his inmost heart that the best thing about him was the favor of the worthless fribble whom he governed.

Through all the vicissitudes of Spanish history the force of these married superstitions—reverence for the Church as distinguished from the fear of God, and reverence for the king as distinguished from respect for law—have been the ruling characteristics of the Spanish mind. Among the fatal effects of this has been the extinction of rational piety and rational patriotism. If a man was not a good Catholic he was pretty sure to be an atheist. If he did not honor the king he was an outlaw. The wretched story of Spanish dissensions beyond seas, and the loss of the vast American empire, is distinctly traceable to the exaggerated sentiment of personal honor, unrestrained by the absolute authority of the crown. It seems impossible for the Spaniard of history and tradition to obey anything out of his sight. The American provinces have been lost one by one through petty quarrels and colonial rivalries. At the first word of dispute their notion of honor obliges them to fly to arms, and when blood has been shed reconciliation is impossible. So weak is the principle of territorial loyalty, that whenever the Peninsula government finds it necessary to overrule some violence of its own soldiers, these find no difficulty in marching over to the insurrection, or raising a fresh rebellion of their own. So little progress has there been in Spain from the middle ages to to-day in true political science, that we see such butchers as Caballero and Valmaseda repeating to-day the crimes and follies of Cortes and Pamfilo Narvaez, of Pizarro and Almagro, and the revolt of the bloodthirsty volunteers of the Havana is only a question of time.

It is true that in later years there has been the beginning of a better system of thought and discussion in Spain. But the old tradition still holds its own gallantly in Church and state. Nowhere in the world are the forms of religion so rigidly observed, and the precepts of Christian morality less regarded. The most facile beauties in Madrid are severe as Minervas on Holy Thursday. I have seen a dozen fast men at the door of a gambling-house fall on their knees in the dust as the Host passed by in the street. Yet the fair were no less frail and the senoritos were no less profligate for this unfeigned reverence for the outside of the cup and platter.

In the domain of politics there is still the lamentable disproportion between honor and honesty. A high functionary cares nothing if the whole Salon del Prado talks of his pilferings, but he will risk his life in an instant if you call him no gentleman. The word "honor" is still used in all legislative assemblies, even in England and America. But the idea has gone by the board in all democracies, and the word means no more than the chamberlain's sword or the speaker's mace. The only criterion which the statesman of the nineteenth century applies to public acts is that of expediency and legality. The first question is, "Is it lawful?" the second, "Does it pay?" Both of these are questions of fact, and as such susceptible of discussion and proof. The question of honor and religion carries us at once into the realm of sentiment where no demonstration is possible. But this is where every question is planted from the beginning in Spanish politics. Every public matter presents itself under this form: "Is it consistent with Spanish honor?" and "Will it be to the advantage of the Roman Catholic Apostolic Church?" Now, nothing is consistent with Spanish honor which does not recognize the Spain of to-day as identical with the Spain of the sixteenth century, and the bankrupt government of Madrid as equal in authority to the world-wide autocracy of Charles V. And nothing is thought to be to the advantage of the Church which does not tend to the concubinage of the spiritual and temporal power, and to the muzzling of speech and the drugging of the mind to sleep.

Let any proposition be made which touches this traditional susceptibility of race, no matter how sensible or profitable it may be, and you hear in the Cortes and the press, and, louder than all, among the idle cavaliers of the *cafes,* the wildest denunciations of the treason that would consent to look at things as they are. The men who have ventured to support the common-sense view are speedily stormed into silence or timid self-defence. The sword of Guzman is brandished in the Chambers, the name of Pelayo is invoked, the memory of the Cid is awakened, and the proposition goes out in a blaze of patriotic pyrotechnics, to the intense satisfaction of the unthinking and the grief of the judicious. The senoritos go back to the serious business of their lives—coffee and cigarettes—with a genuine glow of pride in a country which is capable of the noble self-sacrifice of cutting off its nose to spite somebody else's face.

But I repeat, the most favorable sign of the times is that this tyranny of tradition is losing its power. A great deal was done by the single act of driving out the queen. This was a blow at superstition which gave to the whole body politic a most salutary shock. Never before in Spain had a revolution been directed at the throne. Before it was always an obnoxious ministry that was to be driven out. The monarch remained; and the exiled outlaw of to-day might be premier to-morrow. But the fall of Novaliches at the Bridge of Alcolea decided the fate not only of the ministry but of the dynasty; and while General Concha was waiting for the train to leave Madrid, Isabel of Bourbon and Divine Right were passing the Pyrenees.

Although the moral power of the Church is still so great, the incorporation of freedom of worship in the constitution of 1869 has been followed by a really remarkable development of freedom of thought. The proposition was regarded by some with horror and by others with contempt. One of the most enlightened statesmen in Spain once said to me, "The provision for freedom of worship in the constitution is a mere abstract proposition,—it can never have any practical value except for foreigners. I cannot conceive of a Spaniard being anything but a Catholic." And so powerful was this impression in the minds of the deputies that the article only accords freedom of worship to foreigners in Spain, and adds, hypothetically, that if any Spaniards should profess any other religion than the Catholic, they are entitled to the same liberty as foreigners. The Inquisition has been dead half a century, but you can see how its ghost still haunts the official mind of Spain. It is touching to see how the broken links of the chain of superstition still hang about even those who imagine they are defying it. As in their Christian burials, following unwittingly the example of the hated Moors, they bear the corpse with uncovered face to the grave, and follow it with the funeral torch of the Romans, so the formula of the Church clings even to the mummery of the atheists. Not long ago in Madrid a man and woman who belonged to some fantastic order which rejected religion and law had a child born to them in the course of things, and determined that it should begin life free from the taint of superstition. It should not be christened, it should be named, in the Name of Reason. But they could not break loose from the idea of baptism. They poured a bottle of water on the shivering nape of the poor little neophyte, and its frail life went out in its first wheezing week.

But in spite of all this a spirit of religious inquiry is growing up in Spain, and the Church sees it and cannot prevent it. It watches the liberal newspapers and the Protestant prayer-meetings much as the old giant in Bunyan's dream glared at the passing pilgrims, mumbling and muttering toothless curses. It looks as if the dead sleep of uniformity of thought were to be broken at last, and Spain were to enter the healthful and vivifying atmosphere of controversy.

Symptoms of a similar change may be seen in the world of politics. The Republican party is only a year or two old, but what a vigorous and noisy infant it is! With all its faults and errors, it seems to have the promise of a sturdy and wholesome future. It refuses to be bound by the memories of the past, but keeps its eyes fixed on the brighter possibilities to come. Its journals, undeterred by the sword of Guzman or the honor of all the Caballeros,—the men on horseback,—are advocating such sensible measures as justice to the Antilles, and the sale of outlying property, which costs more than it produces. Emilio Castelar, casting behind him all the restraints of tradition, announces as his idea of liberty "the right of all citizens to obey nothing but the law." There is no sounder doctrine than this preached in Manchester or Boston. If the Spanish people can be brought to see that God is greater than the Church, and that the law is above the king, the day of final deliverance is at hand.

TAUROMACHY

The bull-fight is the national festival of Spain. The rigid Britons have had their fling at it for many years. The effeminate *badaud* of Paris has declaimed against its barbarity. Even the aristocracy of Spain has begun to suspect it of vulgarity and to withdraw from the arena the light of its noble countenance. But the Spanish people still hold it to their hearts and refuse to be weaned from it.

"As Panem et Circenses was the cry Among the Roman populace of old, So
Pan y Toros is the cry in Spain."

It is a tradition which has passed into their national existence. They received it from nowhere. They have transmitted it nowhither except to their own colonies. In late years an effort has been made to transplant it, but with small success. There were a few bull-fights four years ago at Havre. There was a sensation of curiosity which soon died away. This year in London the experiment was tried, but was hooted out of existence, to the great displeasure of the Spanish journals, who said the ferocious Islanders would doubtless greatly prefer baiting to death a half dozen Irish serfs from the estate of Lord Fritters, — a gentle diversion in which we are led to believe the British peers pass their leisure hours.

It is this monopoly of the bull-fight which so endears it to the Spanish heart. It is to them conclusive proof of the vast superiority of both the human and taurine species in Spain. The eminent torero, Pepe Illo, said: "The love of bulls is inherent in man, especially in the Spaniard, among which glorious people there have been bull-fights ever since bulls were, because," adds Pepe, with that modesty which forms so charming a trait of the Iberian character, "the Spanish men are as much more brave than all other men, as the Spanish bull is more savage and valiant than all other bulls."

The sport permeates the national life. I have seen it woven into the tapestry of palaces, and rudely stamped on the handkerchief of the peasant. It is the favorite game of children in the street. Loyal Spain was thrilled with joy recently on reading in its Paris correspondence that when the exiled Prince of Asturias went for a half-holiday to visit his imperial comrade at the Tuileries, the urchins had a game of "toro" on the terrace, admirably conducted by the little Bourbon and followed up with great spirit by the little Montijo-Bonaparte.

The bull-fight has not always enjoyed the royal favor. Isabel the Catholic would fain have abolished bathing and bull-fighting together. The Spaniards, who willingly gave up their ablutions, stood stoutly by their bulls, and the energetic queen was baffled. Again when the Bourbons came in with Philip V., the courtiers turned up their thin noses at the coarse diversion, and induced the king to abolish it. It would not stay abolished, however, and Philip's successor built the present coliseum in expiation. The spectacle has, nevertheless, lost much of its early splendor by the hammering of time. Formerly the gayest and bravest gentlemen of the court, mounted on the best horses in the kingdom, went into the arena and defied the bull in the names of their lady-loves. Now the bull is baited and slain by hired artists, and the horses they mount are the sorriest hacks that ever went to the knacker.

One of the most brilliant shows of the kind that was ever put upon the scene was the Festival of Bulls given by Philip IV. in honor of Charles I.,

"When the Stuart came from far,
Led by his love's sweet pain,
To Mary, the guiding star
That shone in the heaven of Spain."

And the memory of that dazzling occasion was renewed by Ferdinand VII. in the year of his death, when he called upon his subjects to swear allegiance to his baby Isabel. This festival took place in the Plaza Mayor. The king and court occupied the same balconies which Charles and his royal friend and model had filled two centuries before. The champions were poor nobles, of good blood but scanty substance, who fought for glory and pensions, and had quadrilles of well-trained bull-fighters at their stirrups to prevent the farce from becoming tragedy. The royal life of Isabel of Bourbon was inaugurated by the spilled blood of one hundred bulls save one. The gory prophecy of that day has been well sustained. Not one year has passed since then free from blood shed in her cause.

But these extraordinary attractions are not necessary to make a festival of bulls the most seductive of all pleasures to a Spaniard. On any pleasant Sunday afternoon, from Easter to All Souls, you have only to go into the street to see that there is some great excitement fusing the populace into one living mass of sympathy. All faces are turned one way, all minds are filled with one purpose. From the Puerta del Sol down the wide Alcala a vast crowd winds, solid as a glacier and bright as a kaleidoscope. From the grandee in his bla-zoned carriage to the manola in her calico gown, there is no class unrepresented. Many a red hand grasps the magic ticket which is to open the realm of enchantment to-day, and which represents short commons for a week before. The pawnbrokers' shops have been very animated for the few preceding days. There is nothing too precious to be parted with for the sake of the bulls. Many of these smart girls have made the ultimate sacrifice for that coveted scrap of paper. They would leave one their mother's cross with the children of Israel rather than not go. It is no cheap entertainment. The worst places in the broiling sun cost twenty cents, four reals; and the box-es are sold usually at fifteen dollars. These prices are necessary to cover the heavy expenses of bulls, horses, and gladiators.

The way to the bull-ring is one of indescribable animation. The cabmen drive furiously this day their broken-kneed nags, who will soon be found on the horns of the bulls, for this is the natural death of the Madrid cab-horse; the omnibus teams dash gayly along with their shrill chime of bells; there are the rude jests of clowns and the high voices of excited girls; the water-venders droning their tempt-ing cry, "Cool as the snow!" the sellers of fans and the merchants of gingerbread picking up their harvests in the hot and hungry crowd.

The Plaza de Toros stands just outside the monumental gate of the Alcala. It is a low, squat, prison-like circus of stone, stuccoed and whitewashed, with no pretence of ornament or architectural effect. There is no nonsense whatever about it. It is built for the killing of bulls and for no other purpose. Around it, on a day of battle, you will find encamped great armies of the lower class of Madrilenos, who, being at financial ebb-tide, cannot pay to go in. But they come all the same, to be in the enchanted neighborhood, to hear the shouts and roars of the favored ones within, and to seize any possible occasion for getting in. Who knows? A caballero may come out and give them his check. An English lady may become disgusted and go home, taking away numerous lords whose places will be vacant. The sky may fall, and they may catch four reals' worth of larks. It is worth taking the chances.

One does not soon forget the first sight of the full coliseum. In the centre is the sanded arena, surrounded by a high barrier. Around this rises the graded succession of stone benches for the people; then numbered seats for the connoisseurs; and above a row of boxes extending around the circle. The building holds, when full, some fourteen thousand persons; and there is rarely any vacant space. For myself I can say that what I vainly strove to imagine in the coliseum at Rome, and in the more solemn solitude of the amphitheatres of Capua and Pompeii, came up before me with the vividness of life on entering the bull-ring of Madrid. This, and none other, was the classic arena. This was the crowd that sat expectant, under the blue sky, in the hot glare of the South, while the doomed captives of Dacia or the sectaries of Judea commended their souls to the gods of the Danube, or the Crucified of Galilee. Half the sand lay in the blinding sun. Half the seats were illuminated by the fierce light. The other half was in shadow, and the dark crescent crept slowly all the afternoon across the arena as the sun declined in the west.

It is hard to conceive a more brilliant scene. The women put on their gayest finery for this occasion. In the warm light, every bit of color flashes out, every combination falls naturally into its place. I am afraid the luxuriance of hues in the dress of the fair Iberians would be considered shocking in Broadway, but in the vast frame and broad light of the Plaza the effect was very brilliant. Thousands of party-colored paper fans are sold at the ring. The favorite colors are the national red and yellow, and the fluttering of these broad, bright disks of color is dazzlingly attractive. There is a gayety of conversation, a quick fire of repartee, shouts of recognition and salutation, which altogether make up a bewildering confusion.

The weary young water-men scream their snow-cold refreshment. The orange-men walk with their gold-freighted baskets along the barrier, and throw their oranges with the most marvellous skill and certainty to people in distant boxes or benches. They never miss their mark. They will throw over the heads of a thousand people a dozen oranges into the outstretched hands of customers, so swiftly that it seems like one line of gold from the dealer to the buyer.

At length the blast of a trumpet announces the clearing of the ring. The idlers who have been lounging in the arena are swept out by the alguaciles, and the hum of conversation gives way to an expectant silence. When the last loafer has reluctantly retired, the great gate is thrown open, and the procession of the toreros enters. They advance in a glittering line: first the marshals of the day, then the picadors on horseback, then the matadors on foot surrounded each by his quadrille of chulos. They walk towards the box which holds the city fathers, under whose patronage the show is given, and formally salute the authority. This is all very classic, also, recalling the *Ave Caesar, morituri,* etc., of the gladiators. It lacks, however, the solemnity of the Roman salute, from those splendid fellows who would never all leave the arena alive. A bullfighter is sometimes killed, it is true, but the percentage of deadly danger is scarcely enough to make a spectator's heart beat as the bedizened procession comes flashing by in the sun.

The municipal authority throws the bowing alguacil a key, which he catches in his hat, or is hissed if he misses it. With this he unlocks the door through which the bull is to enter, and then scampers off with undignified haste through the opposite entrance. There is a bugle flourish, the door flies open, and the bull rushes out, blind with the staring light, furious with rage, trembling in every limb. This is the most intense moment of the day. The glorious brute is the target of twelve thousand pairs of eyes. There is a silence as of death, while every one waits to see his first movement. He is doomed from the beginning; the curtain has risen on a three-act tragedy, which will surely end with his death, but the incidents which are to fill the interval are all unknown. The minds and eyes of all that vast assembly know nothing for the time but the movements of that brute. He stands for an instant recovering his senses. He has been shot suddenly out of the darkness into that dazzling light. He sees around him a sight such as he never confronted before,—a wall of living faces lit up by thousands of staring eyes. He does not dwell long upon this, however; in his pride and anger he sees a nearer enemy. The horsemen have taken position near the gate, where they sit motionless as burlesque statues, their long ashen spears, iron-tipped, in rest, their wretched nags standing blindfolded, with trembling knees, and necks like dromedaries, not dreaming of their near fate. The bull rushes, with a snort, at the nearest one. The picador holds firmly, planting his spear-point in the shoulder of the brute. Sometimes the bull flinches at this sharp and sudden punishment, and the picador, by a sudden turn to the left, gets away unhurt. Then there is applause for the torero and hisses for the bull. Some indignant amateurs go so far as to call him cow, and to inform him that he is the son of his mother. But oftener he rushes in, not caring for the spear, and with one toss of his sharp horns tumbles horse and rider in one heap against the barrier and upon the sand. The capeadores, the cloak-bearers, come fluttering around and divert the bull from his prostrate victims. The picador is lifted to his feet,—his iron armor not permitting him to rise without help,—and the horse is rapidly scanned to see if his wounds are immediately mortal. If not, the picador mounts again, and provokes the bull to another rush. A horse will usually endure two or three attacks before dying. Sometimes a single blow from in front pierces the heart, and the blood spouts forth in a cataract. In this case the picador hastily dismounts, and the bridle and saddle are stripped in an instant from the dying brute. If a bull is energetic and rapid in execution, he will clear the arena in a few moments. He rushes at one horse after another, tears them open with his terrible "spears" ("horns" is a word never used in the ring), and sends them madly galloping over the arena, trampling out their gushing bowels as they fly. The assistants watch their opportunity, from time to time, to take the wounded horses out of the ring, plug up their gaping rents with tow, and sew them roughly up for another sally. It is incredible to see what these poor creatures will endure,—carrying their riders at a lumbering gallop over the ring, when their thin sides seem empty of entrails.

Sometimes the bull comes upon the dead body of a horse he has killed. The smell of blood and the unmoving helplessness of the victim excite him to the highest pitch. He gores and tramples the carcass, and tosses it in the air with evident enjoyment, until diverted by some living tormentor. You will occasionally see a picador nervous and anxious about his personal safety. They are ignorant and superstitious, and subject to presentiments; they often go into the ring with the impression that their last hour has come. If one takes counsel of his fears and avoids the shock of combat, the hard-hearted crowd immediately discover it and rain maledictions on his head. I saw a picador once enter the ring as pale as death. He kept carefully out of the way of the bull for a few minutes. The sharp-eyed Spaniards noticed it, and commenced shouting, "Craven! He wants to live forever!" They threw orange-skins at him, and at last, their rage vanquishing their economy, they pelted him with oranges. His pallor gave way to a flush of shame and anger. He attacked the bull so awkwardly that the animal, killing his horse, threw him also with great violence. His hat flew off, his bald head struck the hard soil. He lay there as one dead, and was borne away lifeless. This mollified the indignant people, and they desisted from their abuse.

A cowardly bull is much more dangerous than a courageous one, who lowers his head, shuts his eyes, and goes blindly at everything he sees. The last refuge of a bull in trouble is to leap the barrier, where he produces a lively moment among the water-carriers and orange-boys and stage-carpenters. I once saw a bull, who had done very little execution in the arena, leap the barrier suddenly and toss an unfortunate carpenter from the gangway sheer into the ring. He picked himself up, laughed, saluted his friends, ran a little distance and fell, and was carried out dying. Fatal accidents are rarely mentioned in the newspapers, and it is considered not quite good form to talk about them.

When the bull has killed enough horses, the first act of the play terminates. But this is an exceedingly delicate matter for the authorities to decide. The audience will not endure any economy in this respect. If the bull is enterprising and "voluntary," he must have as many horses as he can dispose of. One day in Madrid the bulls operated with such activity that the supply of horses was exhausted before the close of the show, and the contractors rushed out in a panic and bought a half dozen screws from the nearest cab-stand. If the president orders out the horses before their time, he will hear remarks by no means complimentary from the austere groundlings.

The second act is the play of the banderilleros, the flag-men. They are beautifully dressed and superbly built fellows, principally from Andalusia, got up precisely like Figaro in the opera. Theirs is the most delicate and graceful operation of the bull-fight. They take a pair of barbed darts, with little banners fluttering at their ends, and provoke the bull to rush at them. At the instant he reaches them, when it seems nothing can save them, they step aside and plant the banderillas in the neck of the bull. If the bull has been cowardly and sluggish, and the spectators have called for "fire," darts are used filled with detonating powder at the base, which explode in the flesh of the bull. He dances and skips like a kid or a colt in his agony, which is very diverting to the Spanish mind. A prettier conceit is that of confining small birds in paper cages, which come apart when the banderilla is planted, and set the little fluttering captives free.

Decking the bull with these torturing ornaments is the last stage in the apprenticeship of the chulo, before he rises to the dignity of matador, or killer. The matadors themselves on special occasions think it no derogation from their dignity to act as banderilleros. But they usually accompany the act with some exaggeration of difficulty that reaps for them a harvest of applause. Frascuelo sits in a chair and plants the irritating bannerets. Lagartijo lays his handkerchief on the ground and stands upon it while he coifs the bull. A performance which never fails to bring down the house is for the torero to await the rush of the bull, and when the bellowing monster comes at him with winking eyes and lowered head, to put his slippered foot between the horns, and vault lightly over his back.

These chulos exhibit the most wonderful skill and address in evading the assault of the bull. They can almost always trick him by waving their cloaks a little out of the line of their flight. Sometimes, however, the bull runs straight at the man, disregarding the flag, and if the distance is great to the barrier the danger is imminent; for swift as these men are, the bulls are swifter. Once I saw the bull strike the torero at the instant he vaulted over the barrier. He fell sprawling some distance the other side, safe, but terribly bruised and stunned. As soon as he could collect himself he sprang into the arena again, looking very seedy; and the crowd roared, "Saved by miracle." I could but think of Basilio, who, when the many cried, "A miracle," answered, "Industria! Industria!" But these bullfighters are all very pious, and glad to curry favor with the saints by attributing every success to their intervention. The famous matador, Paco Montes, fervently believed in an amulet he carried, and in the invocation of Our Lord of the True Cross. He called upon this special name in every tight place, and while other people talked of his luck he stoutly affirmed it was his faith that saved him; often he said he saw the veritable picture of the Passion coming down between him and the bull, in answer to his prayers. At every bull-ring there is a little chapel in the refreshment-room where these devout ruffians can toss off a prayer or two in the intervals of work. A priest is always at hand with a consecrated wafer, to visa the torero's passport who has to start suddenly for Paradise. It is not exactly regular, but the ring has built many churches and endowed many chapels, and must not be too rigidly regarded. In many places the chief boxes are reserved for the clergy, and prayers are hurried through an hour earlier on the day of combat.

The final act is the death of the bull. It must come at last. His exploits in the early part of his career afford to the amateur some indication of the manner in which he will meet his end. If he is a generous, courageous brute, with more heart than brains, he will die gallantly and be easily killed. But if he has shown reflection, forethought, and that saving quality of the oppressed, suspicion, the matador has a serious work before him. The bull is always regarded from this objective standpoint. The more power of reason the brute has, the worse opinion the Spaniard has of him. A stupid creature who rushes blindly on the sword of the matador is an animal after his own heart. But if there be one into whose brute brain some glimmer of the awful truth has come, — and this sometimes happens, — if he feels the solemn question at issue between him and his enemy, if he eyes the man and not the flag, if he refuses to be fooled by the waving lure, but keeps all his strength and all his faculties for his own defence, the soul of the Spaniard rises up in hate and loathing. He calls on the matador to kill him any way. If he will not rush at the flag, the crowd shouts for the demi-lune; and the noble brute is houghed from behind, and your soul grows sick with shame of human nature, at the hellish glee with which they watch him hobbling on his severed legs.

This seldom happens. The final act is usually an admirable study of coolness and skill against brute force. When the banderillas are all planted, and the bugles sound for the third time, the matador, the espada, the sword, steps forward with a modest consciousness of distinguished merit, and makes a brief speech to the corregidor, offering in honor of the good city of Madrid to kill the bull. He turns on his heel, throws his hat by a dexterous back-handed movement over the barrier, and advances, sword and cape in hand, to where his noble enemy awaits him. The bull appears to recognize a more serious foe than any he has encountered. He stops short and eyes the newcomer curiously. It is always an impressive picture: the tortured, maddened animal, whose thin flanks are palpitating with his hot breath, his coat one shining mass of blood from the darts and the spear-thrusts, his massive neck still decked as in mockery with the fluttering flags, his fine head and muzzle seeming sharpened by the hour's terrible experience, his formidable horns crimsoned with onset; in front of this fiery bulk of force and courage, the slight, sinewy frame of the killer, whose only reliance is on his coolness and his intellect. I never saw a matador come carelessly to his work. He is usually pale and alert. He studies the bull for a moment with all his eyes. He waves the blood-red engano, or lure, before his face. If the bull rushes at it with his eyes shut, the work is easy. He has only to select his own stroke and make it. But if the bull is jealous and sly, it requires the most careful management to kill him. The disposition of the bull is developed by a few rapid passes of the red flag. This must not be continued too long: the tension of the nerves of the auditory will not bear trifling. I remember one day the crowd was aroused to fury by a bugler from the adjoining barracks playing retreat at the moment of decision. All at once the matador seizes the favorable instant. He poises his sword as the bull rushes upon him. The point enters just between the left shoulder and the spine; the long blade glides in up to the hilt. The bull reels and staggers and dies. Sometimes the matador severs the vertebrae. The effect is like magic. He lays the point of his sword between the bull's horns, as lightly as a lady who touches her cavalier with her fan, and he falls dead as a stone.

If the blow is a clean, well-delivered one, the enthusiasm of the people is unbounded. Their approval comes up in a thunderous shout of "Well done! Valiente! Viva!" A brown shower of cigars rains on the sand. The victor gathers them up: they fill his hands, his pockets, his hat. He gives them to his friends, and the aromatic shower continues. Hundreds of hats are flung into the ring. He picks them up and shies them back to their shouting owners. Sometimes a dollar is mingled with the flying compliments; but the enthusiasm of the Spaniard rarely carries him so far as that. For ten minutes after a good estocada, the matador is the most popular man in Spain.

But the trumpets sound again, the door of the Toril flies open, another bull comes rushing out, and the present interest quenches the past. The play begins again, with its sameness of purpose and its infinite variety of incident.

It is not quite accurate to say, as is often said, that the bull-fighter runs no risk. El Tato, the first sword of Spain, lost his leg in 1869, and his life was saved by the coolness and courage of Lagartijo, who succeeded him in the championship, and who was terribly wounded in the foot the next summer. Arjona killed a bull in the same year, which tossed and ruptured him after receiving his death-blow. Pepe Illo died in harness, on the sand. Every year picadors, chulos, and such small deer are killed, without gossip. I must copy the inscription on the sword which Tato presented to Lagartijo, as a specimen of tauromachian literature: —

"If, as philosophers say, gratitude is the tribute of noble souls, accept, dear Lagartijo, this present; preserve it as a sacred relic, for it symbolizes the memory of my glories, and is at the same time the mute witness of my misfortune. With it I killed my last bull named *Peregrino,* bred by D. Vicente Martinez, fourth of the fight of the 7th June, 1869, in which act I received the wound which has caused the amputation of my right leg. The will of man can do nothing against the designs of Providence. Nothing but resignation is left to thy affectionate friend, Antonio Sanchez [Tato]."

It is in consideration of the mingled skill and danger of the trade, that such enormous fees are paid the principal performers. The leading swordsmen receive about three hundred dollars for each performance, and they are eagerly disputed by the direction of all the arenas of Spain. In spite of these large wages, they are rarely rich. They are as wasteful and improvident as gamblers. Tato, when he lost his leg, lost his means of subsistence, and his comrades organized one or two benefits to keep him from want. Cuchares died in the Havana, and left no provision for his family.

There is a curious naivete in the play-bill of a bull-fight, the only conscientious public document I have seen in Spain. You know how we of Northern blood exaggerate the attractions of all sorts of shows, trusting to the magnanimity of the audience. "He warn't nothing like so little as that," confesses Mr. Magsman, "but where's your dwarf what is?" There are few who have the moral courage to demand their money back because they counted but thirty-nine thieves when the bills promised forty. But the management of the Madrid bull-ring knows its public too well to promise more than it is sure of performing. It announces six bulls, and positively no more. It says there will be no use of bloodhounds. It promises two picadors, with three others in reserve, and warns the public that if all five become inutilized in the combat, no more will be issued. With so fair a preliminary statement, what crowd, however inflammable, could mob the management?

Some industrious and ascetic statistician has visited Spain and interested himself in the bullring. Here are some of the results of his researches. In 1864 the number of places in all the taurine establishments of Spain was 509,283, of which 246,813 belonged to the cities, and 262,470 to the country.

In the year 1864, there were 427 bull-fights, of which 294 took place in the cities, and 13 3 in the country towns. The receipts of ninety-eight bullrings in 1864 reached the enormous sum of two hundred and seventeen and a half millions of reals (nearly $11,000,000). The 427 bull-fights which took place in Spain during the year 1864 caused the death of 2989 of these fine animals, and about 7473 horses,—something more than half the number of the cavalry of Spain. These wasted victims could have ploughed three hundred thousand hectares of land, which would have produced a million and a half hectolitres of grain, worth eighty millions of reals; all this without counting the cost of the slaughtered cattle, worth say seven or eight millions, at a moderate calculation.

Thus far the Arithmetic Man; to whom responds the tauromachian aficionado: That the bulk of this income goes to purposes of charity; that were there no bull-fights, bulls of good race would cease to be bred; that nobody ever saw a horse in a bull-ring that could plough a furrow of a hundred yards without giving up the ghost; that the nerve, dexterity, and knowledge of brute nature gained in the arena is a good thing to have in the country; that, in short, it is our way of amusing ourselves, and if you don't like it you can go home and cultivate prize-fighters, or kill two-year-old colts on the racecourse, or murder jockeys in hurdle-races, or break your own necks in steeple-chases, or in search of wilder excitement thicken your blood with beer or burn your souls out with whiskey.

And this is all we get by our well-meant effort to convince Spaniards of the brutality of bullfights. Must Chicago be virtuous before I can object to Madrid ale, and say that its cakes are unduly gingered?

Yet even those who most stoutly defend the bull-fight feel that its glory has departed and that it has entered into the era of full decadence. I was talking one evening with a Castilian gentleman, one of those who cling with most persistence to the national traditions, and he confessed that the noble art was wounded to death. "I do not refer, as many do, to the change from the old times, when gentlemen fought on their own horses in the ring. That was nonsense, and could not survive the time of Cervantes. Life is too short to learn bull-fighting. A grandee of Spain, if he knows anything else, would make a sorry torero. The good times of the art are more modern. I saw the short day of the glory of the ring when I was a boy. There was a race of gladiators then, such as the world will never see again,—mighty fighters before the king. Pepe Illo and Costillares, Romero and Paco Montes,—the world does not contain the stuff to make their counterparts. They were serious, earnest men. They would have let their right arms wither before they would have courted the applause of the mob by killing a bull outside of the severe traditions. Compare them with the men of to-day, with your Rafael Molina, who allows himself to be gored, playing with a heifer; with your frivolous boys like Frascuelo. I have seen the ring convulsed with laughter as that buffoon strutted across the arena, flirting his muleta as a manola does her skirts, the bewildered bull not knowing what to make of it. It was enough to make Illo turn in his bloody grave.

"Why, my young friend, I remember when bulls were a dignified and serious matter; when we kept account of their progress from their pasture to the capital. We had accounts of their condition by couriers and carrier-pigeons. On the day when they appeared it was a high festival in the court. All the sombreros in Spain were there, the ladies in national dress with white mantillas. The young queen always in her palco (may God guard her). The fighters of that day were high priests of art; there was something of veneration in the regard that was paid them. Duchesses threw them bouquets with billets-doux. Gossip and newspapers have destroyed the romance of common life.

"The only pleasure I take in the Plaza de Toros now is at night. The custodians know me and let me moon about in the dark. When all that is ignoble and mean has faded away with the daylight, it seems to me the ghosts of the old time come back upon the sands. I can fancy the patter of light hoofs, the glancing of spectral horns. I can imagine the agile tread of Romero, the deadly thrust of Montes, the whisper of long-vanished applause, and the clapping of ghostly hands. I am growing too old for such skylarking, and I sometimes come away with a cold in my head. But you will never see a bull-fight you can enjoy as I do these visionary festivals, where memory is the corregidor, and where the only spectators are the stars and I."

RED-LETTER DAYS

No people embrace more readily than the Spaniards the opportunity of spending a day without work. Their frequent holidays are a relic of the days when the Church stood between the people and their taskmasters, and fastened more firmly its hold upon the hearts of the ignorant and overworked masses, by becoming at once the fountain of salvation in the next world, and of rest in this. The government rather encouraged this growth of play-days, as the Italian Bourbons used to foster mendicancy, by way of keeping the people as unthrifty as possible. Lazzaroni are so much more easily managed than burghers!

It is only the holy days that are successfully celebrated in Spain. The state has tried of late years to consecrate to idle parade a few revolutionary dates, but they have no vigorous national life. They grow feebler and more colorless year by year, because they have no depth of earth.

The most considerable of these national festivals is the 2d of May, which commemorates the slaughter of patriots in the streets of Madrid by Murat. This is a political holiday which appeals more strongly to the national character of the Spaniards than any other. The mingled pride of race and ignorant hate of everything foreign which constitutes that singular passion called Spanish patriotism, or Espanolismo, is fully called into play by the recollections of the terrible scenes of their war of independence, which drove out a foreign king, and brought back into Spain a native despot infinitely meaner and more injurious. It is an impressive study in national character and thought, this self-satisfaction of even liberal Spaniards at the reflection that, by a vast and supreme effort of the nation, after countless sacrifices and with the aid of coalesced Europe, they exchanged Joseph Bonaparte for Ferdinand VII. and the Inquisition. But the victims of the Dos de Mayo fell fighting. Daoiz, Velarde, and Ruiz were bayoneted at their guns, scorning surrender. The alcalde of Mostoles, a petty village of Castile, called on Spain to rise against the tyrant. And Spain obeyed the summons of this cross-roads justice. The contempt of probabilities, the Quixotism of these successive demonstrations, endear them to the Spanish heart.

Every 2d of May the city of Madrid gives up the day to funeral honors to the dead of 1808. The city government, attended by its Maceros, in their gorgeous robes of gold and scarlet, with silver maces and long white plumes; the public institutions of all grades, with invalids and veterans and charity children; a large detachment of the army and navy,—form a vast procession at the Town Hall, and, headed by the Supreme Government, march to slow music through the Puerta del Sol and the spacious Alcala street to the granite obelisk in the Prado which marks the resting-place of the patriot dead. I saw the regent of the kingdom, surrounded by his cabinet, sauntering all a summer's afternoon under a blazing sun over the dusty mile that separates the monument from the Ayuntamiento. The Spaniards are hopelessly inefficient in these matters. The people always fill the line of march, and a rivulet of procession meanders feebly through a wilderness of mob. It is fortunate that the crowd is more entertaining than the show.

The Church has a very indifferent part in this ceremonial. It does nothing more than celebrate a mass in the shade of the dark cypresses in the Place of Loyalty, and then leaves the field clear to the secular power. But this is the only purely civic ceremony I ever saw in Spain. The Church is lord of the holidays for the rest of the year.

In the middle of May comes the feast of the ploughboy patron of Madrid,—San Isidro. He was a true Madrileno in tastes, and spent his time lying in the summer shade or basking in the winter sunshine, seeing visions, while angels came down from heaven and did his farm chores for him. The angels are less amiable nowadays, but every true child of Madrid reveres the example and envies the success of the San Isidro method of doing business. In the process of years this lazy lout has become a great saint, and his bones have done more extensive and remarkable miracle-work than any equal amount of phosphate in existence. In desperate cases of sufficient rank the doctors throw up the sponge and send for Isidro's urn, and the drugging having ceased, the noble patient frequently recovers, and much honor and profit comes thereby to the shrine of the saint.

There is something of the toady in Isidro's composition. You never hear of his curing any one of less than princely rank. I read in an old chronicle of Madrid, that once when Queen Isabel the Catholic was hunting in the hills that overlook the Manzanares, near what is now the oldest and quaintest quarter of the capital, she killed a bear of great size and ferocity; and doubtless thinking it might not be considered lady-like to have done it unassisted, she gave San Isidro the credit of the lucky blow and built him a nice new chapel for it near the Church of San Andres. If there are any doubters, let them go and see the chapel, as I did. When the allied armies of the Christian kings of Spain were seeking for a passage through the hills to the Plains of Tolosa, a shepherd appeared and led them straight to victory and endless fame. After the battle, which broke the Moorish power forever in Central Spain, instead of looking for the shepherd and paying him handsomely for his timely scout-service, they found it more pious and economical to say it was San Isidro in person who had kindly made himself flesh for this occasion. By the great altar in the Cathedral of Toledo stand side by side the statues of Alonso VIIL, the Christian commander, and San Isidro brazenly swelling in the shepherd garb of that unknown guide who led Alonso and his chivalry through the tangled defiles of the Sierra Morena.

His fete is the Derby Day of Madrid. The whole town goes out to his Hermitage on the further banks of the Manzanares, and spends a day or two of the soft spring weather in noisy frolic. The little church stands on a bare brown hill, and all about it is an improvised village consisting half of restaurants and the other half of toyshops. The principal traffic is in a pretty sort of glass whistle which forms the stem of an artificial rose, worn in the button-hole in the intervals of tooting, and little earthen pig-bells, whose ringing scares away the lightning. There is but one duty of the day to flavor all its pleasures. The faithful must go into the oratory, pay a penny, and kiss a glass-covered relic of the saint which the attendant ecclesiastic holds in his hand. The bells are rung violently until the church is full; then the doors are shut and the kissing begins. They are very expeditious about it. The worshippers drop on their knees by platoons before the railing. The long-robed relic-keeper puts the precious trinket rapidly to their lips; an acolyte follows with a saucer for the cash.

The glass grows humid with many breaths. The priest wipes it with a dirty napkin from time to time. The multitude advances, kisses, pays, and retires, till all have their blessing; then the doors are opened and they all pass out, — the bells ringing furiously for another detachment. The pleasures of the day are like those of all fairs and public merrymaking. Working-people come to be idle, and idle people come to have something to do. There is much eating and little drinking. The milk-stalls are busier than the wine-shops. The people are gay and jolly, but very decent and clean and orderly. To the east of the Hermitage, over and beyond the green cool valley, the city rises on its rocky hills, its spires shining in the cloudless blue. Below on the emerald meadows there are the tents and wagons of those who have come from a distance to the Romeria. The sound of guitars and the drone of peasant songs come up the hill, and groups of men are leaping in the wild barbaric dances of Iberia. The scene is of another day and time. The Celt is here, lord of the land. You can see these same faces at Donnybrook Fair. These large-mouthed, short-nosed, rosy-cheeked peasant-girls are called Dolores and Catalina, but they might be called Bridget and Kathleen. These strapping fellows, with long simian upper lips, with brown leggings and patched, mud-colored overcoats, who are leaping and swinging their cudgels in that Pyrrhic round are as good Tipperary boys as ever mobbed an agent or pounded, twenty to one, a landlord to death. The same unquestioning, fervent faith, the same superficial good-nature, the same facility to be amused, and at bottom the same cowardly and cruel blood-thirst. What is this mysterious law of race which is stronger than time, or varying climates, or changing institutions? Which is cause, and which is effect, race or religion?

The great Church holiday of the year is Corpus Christi. On this day the Host is carried in solemn procession through the principal streets, attended by the high officers of state, several battalions of each arm of the service in fresh bright uniforms, and a vast array of ecclesiastics in the most gorgeous stoles and chasubles their vestiary contains. The windows along the line of march are gayly decked with flags and tapestry. Work is absolutely suspended, and the entire population dons its holiday garb. The Puerta del Sol — at this season blazing with relentless light — is crowded with patient

Madrilenos in their best clothes, the brown-cheeked maidens with flowing silks as in a ball-room, and with no protection against the ardent sky but the fluttering fan they hold in their ungloved hands. As everything is behind time in this easy-going land, there are two or three hours of broiling gossip on the glowing pavement before the Sacred Presence is announced by the ringing of silver bells. As the superb structure of filigree gold goes by, a movement of reverent worship vibrates through the crowd. Forgetful of silks and broadcloth and gossip, they fall on their knees in one party-colored mass, and, bowing their heads and beating their breasts, they mutter their mechanical prayers. There are thinking men who say these shows are necessary; that the Latin mind must see with bodily eyes the thing it worships, or the worship will fade away from its heart. If there were no cathedrals and masses, they say, there would be no religion; if there were no king, there would be no law. But we should not accept too hurriedly this ethnological theory of necessity, which would reject all principles of progress and positive good, and condemn half the human race to perpetual childhood. There was a time when we Anglo-Saxons built cathedrals and worshipped the king. Look at Salisbury and Lincoln and Ely; read the history of the growth of parliaments. There is nothing more beautifully sensuous than the religious spirit that presided over those master works of English Gothic; there is nothing in life more abject than the relics of the English love and fear of princes. But the steady growth of centuries has left nothing but the outworn shell of the old religion and the old loyalty. The churches and the castles still exist. The name of the king still is extant in the constitution. They remain as objects of taste and tradition, hallowed by a thousand memories of earlier days, but, thanks be to God who has given us the victory, the English race is now incapable of making a new cathedral or a new king.

Let us not in our safe egotism deny to others the possibility of a like improvement.

This summery month of June is rich in saints. The great apostles, John, Peter, and Paul, have their anniversaries on its closing days, and the shortest nights of the year are given up to the riotous eating of fritters in their honor. I am afraid that the progress of luxury and love of ease has wrought a change in the observance of these festivals. The feast of midsummer night is called the Verbena of St. John, which indicates that it was formerly a morning solemnity, as the vervain could not be hunted by the youths and maidens of Spain with any success or decorum at midnight. But of late years it may be that this useful and fragrant herb has disappeared from the tawny hills of Castile. It is sure that midsummer has grown too warm for any field work. So that the Madrilenos may be pardoned for spending the day napping, and swarming into the breezy Prado in the light of moon and stars and gas. The Prado is ordinarily the promenade of the better classes, but every Spanish family has its John, Paul, and Peter, and the crowded barrios of Toledo and the Penuelas pour out their ragged hordes to the popular festival. The scene has a strange gypsy wildness. From the round point of Atocha to where Cybele, throned among spouting waters, drives southward her spanking team of marble lions, the park is filled with the merry roysterers. At short intervals are the busy groups of fritter merchants; over the crackling fire a great caldron of boiling oil; beside it a mighty bowl of dough. The bunolero, with the swift precision of machinery, dips his hand into the bowl and makes a delicate ring of the tough dough, which he throws into the bubbling caldron. It remains but a few seconds, and his grimy acolyte picks it out with a long wire and throws it on the tray for sale. They are eaten warm, the droning cry continually sounding, "Bunuelos! Calientitos!" There must be millions of these oily dainties consumed on every night of the Verbena. For the more genteel revellers, the Don Juans, Pedros, and Pablos of the better sort, there are improvised restaurants built of pine planks after sunset and gone before sunrise. But the greater number are bought and eaten by the loitering crowd from the tray of the fritterman. It is like a vast gitano-camp. The hurrying crowd which is going nowhere, the blazing fires, the cries of the venders, the songs of the majos under the great trees of the Paseo, the purposeless hurly-burly, and above, the steam of the boiling oil and the dust raised by the myriad feet, form together a striking and vivid picture. The city is more than usually quiet. The stir of life is localized in the Prado. The only busy men in town are those who stand by the seething oil-pots and manufacture the brittle forage of the browsing herds. It is a jealous business, and requires the undivided attention of its professors. The *ne sutor ultra crepidam* of Spanish proverb is "Bunolero haz tus bunuelos,"—Fritterman, mind thy fritters. With the long days and cooler airs of the autumn begin the different fairs. These are relics of the times of tyranny and exclusive privilege, when for a few days each year, by the intervention of the Church, or as a reward for civic service, full liberty of barter and sale was allowed to all citizens. This custom, more or less modified, may be found in most cities of Europe. The boulevards of Paris swarm with little booths at Christmas-time, which begin and end their lawless commercial life within the week. In Vienna, in Leipsic, and other cities, the same waste-weir of irregular trade is periodically opened. These fairs begin in Madrid with the autumnal equinox, and continue for some weeks in October. They disappear from the Alcala to break out with renewed virulence in the avenue of Atocha, and girdle the city at last with a belt of booths. While they last they give great animation and spirit to the street life of the town. You can scarcely make your way among the heaps of gaudy shawls and handkerchiefs, cheap laces and illegitimate jewels, that cumber the pavement. When the Jews were driven out of Spain, they left behind the true genius of bargaining.

A nut-brown maid is attracted by a brilliant red and yellow scarf. She asks the sleepy merchant nodding before his wares, "What is this rag worth?"

He answers with profound indifference, "Ten reals."

"Hombre! Are you dreaming or crazy?" She drops the coveted neck-gear, and moves on, apparently horror-stricken.

The chapman calls her back peremptorily. "Don't be rash! The scarf is worth twenty reals, but for the sake of Santisima Maria I offered it to you for half price. Very well! You are not suited. What will you give?"

"Caramba! Am I buyer and seller as well? The thing is worth three reals; more is a robbery."

"Jesus! Maria! Jose! and all the family! Go thou with God! We cannot trade. Sooner than sell for less than eight reals I will raise the cover of my brains! Go thou! It is eight of the morning, and still thou dreamest."

She lays down the scarf reluctantly, saying, "Five?"

But the outraged mercer snorts scornfully, "Eight is my last word! Go to!"

She moves away, thinking how well that scarf would look in the Apollo
Gardens, and casts over her shoulder a Parthian glance and bid, "Six!"

"Take it! It is madness, but I cannot waste my time in bargaining."

Both congratulate themselves on the operation. He would have taken five, and she would have given seven. How trade would suffer if we had windows in our breasts!

The first days of November are consecrated to all the saints, and to the souls of all the blessed dead. They are observed in Spain with great solemnity; but as the cemeteries are generally of the dreariest character, bare, bleak, and most forbidding under the ashy sky of the late autumn, the days are deprived of that exquisite sentiment that pervades them in countries where the graves of the dead are beautiful. There is nothing more touching than these offerings of memory you see every year in Mont Parnasse and Pere-la-Chaise. Apart from all beliefs, there is a mysterious influence for good exerted upon the living by the memory of the beloved dead. On all hearts not utterly corrupt, the thoughts that come by the graves of the departed fall like dew from heaven, and quicken into life purer and higher resolves.

In Spain, where there is nothing but desolation in graveyards, the churches are crowded instead, and the bereaved survivors commend to God their departed friends and their own stricken hearts in the dim and perfumed aisles of temples made with hands. A taint of gloom thus rests upon the recollection and the prayer, far different from the consolation that comes with the free air and the sunshine, and the infinite blue vault, where Nature conspires with revelation to comfort and cherish and console.

Christmas apparently comes in Spain on no other mission than that referred to in the old English couplet, "bringing good cheer." The Spaniards are the most frugal of people, but during the days that precede their Noche Buena, their Good Night, they seem to be given up as completely to cares of the commissariat as the most eupeptic of Germans. Swarms of turkeys are driven in from the surrounding country, and taken about the streets by their rustic herdsmen, making the roads gay with their scarlet wattles, and waking rural memories by their vociferous gobbling. The great market-place of the season is the Plaza Mayor. The ever-fruitful provinces of the South are laid under contribution, and the result is a wasteful show of tropical luxuriance that seems most incongruous under the wintry sky. There are mountains of oranges and dates, brown hillocks of nuts of every kind, store of every product of this versatile soil. The air is filled with nutty and fruity fragrance. Under the ancient arcades are the stalls of the butchers, rich with the mutton of Castile, the hams of Estremadura, and the hero-nourishing bull-beef of Andalusian pastures.

At night the town is given up to harmless racket. Nowhere has the tradition of the Latin Saturnalia been fitted with less change into the Christian calendar. Men, women, and children of the proletariat—the unemancipated slaves of necessity—go out this night to cheat their misery with noisy frolic. The owner of a tambourine is the equal of a peer; the proprietor of a guitar is the captain of his hundred. They troop through the dim city with discordant revel and song. They have little idea of music. Every one sings and sings ill. Every one dances, without grace or measure. Their music is a modulated howl of the East. Their dancing is the savage leaping of barbarians. There is no lack of couplets, religious, political, or amatory. I heard one ragged woman with a brown baby at her breast go shrieking through the Street of the Magdalen,—

"This is the eve of Christmas,
No sleep from now till morn,
The Virgin is in travail,
At twelve will the child be born!"

Behind her stumped a crippled beggar, who croaked in a voice rough with frost and aguardiente his deep disillusion and distrust of the great:—

"This is the eve of Christmas,
But what is that to me?

We are ruled by thieves and robbers,
  As it was and will always be."

Next comes a shouting band of the youth of Spain, strapping boys with bushy locks, crisp and black almost to blueness, and gay young girls with flexible forms and dark Arab eyes that shine with a phosphorescent light in the shadows. They troop on with clacking castinets. The challenge of the mozos rings out on the frosty air, —

"This is the eve of Christmas,
Let us drink and love our fill!"

And the saucy antiphon of girlish voices responds, —

"A man may be bearded and gray,
But a woman can fool him still!"

The Christmas and New-Year's holidays continue for a fortnight, ending with the Epiphany. On the eve of the Day of the Kings a curious farce is performed by bands of the lowest orders of the people, which demonstrates the apparently endless naivete of their class. In every coterie of water-carriers, or mozos de cordel, there will be one found innocent enough to believe that the Magi are coming to Madrid that night, and that a proper respect to their rank requires that they must be met at the city gate. To perceive the coming of their feet, beautiful upon the mountains, a ladder is necessary, and the poor victim of the comedy is loaded with this indispensable "property." He is dragged by his gay companions, who never tire of the exquisite wit of their jest, from one gate to another, until suspicion supplants faith in the mind of the neophyte, and the farce is over.

In the burgher society of Castile this night is devoted to a very different ceremony. Each little social circle comes together in a house agreed upon. They take mottoes of gilded paper and write on each the name of some one of the company. The names of the ladies are thrown into one urn, and those of the cavaliers into another, and they are drawn out by pairs. These couples are thus condemned by fortune to intimacy during the year. The gentleman is always to be at the orders of the dame and to serve her faithfully in every knightly fashion. He has all the duties and none of the privileges of a lover, unless it be the joy of those "who stand and wait." The relation is very like that which so astonished M. de Gramont in his visit to Piedmont, where the cavalier of service never left his mistress in public and never approached her in private.

The true Carnival survives in its naive purity only in Spain. It has faded in Rome into a romping day of clown's play. In Paris it is little more than a busier season for dreary and professional vice. Elsewhere all over the world the Carnival gayeties are confined to the salon. But in Madrid the whole city, from grandee to cordwainer, goes with childlike earnestness into the enjoyment of the hour. The Corso begins in the Prado on the last Sunday before Lent, and lasts four days. From noon to night the great drive is filled with a double line of carriages two miles long, and between them are the landaus of the favored hundreds who have the privilege of driving up and down free from the law of the road. This right is acquired by the payment of ten dollars a day to city charities, and produces some fifteen thousand dollars every Carnival. In these carriages all the society of Madrid may be seen; and on foot, darting in and out among the hoofs of the horses, are the young men of Castile in every conceivable variety of absurd and fantastic disguise. There are of course pirates and Indians and Turks, monks, prophets, and kings, but the favorite costumes seem to be the Devil and the Englishman. Sometimes the Yankee is attempted, with indifferent success. He wears a ribbon-wreathed Italian bandit's hat, an embroidered jacket, slashed buckskin trousers, and a wide crimson belt,—a dress you would at once recognize as universal in Boston.

Most of the maskers know by name at least the occupants of the carriages. There is always room for a mask in a coach. They leap in, swarming over the back or the sides, and in their shrill monotonous scream they make the most startling revelations of the inmost secrets of your soul. There is always something impressive in the talk of an unknown voice, but especially is this so in Madrid, where every one scorns his own business, and devotes himself rigorously to his neighbor's. These shrieking young monks and devilkins often surprise a half-formed thought in the heart of a fair Castilian and drag it out into day and derision. No one has the right to be offended. Duchesses are called Tu! Isabel! by chin-dimpled school-boys, and the proudest beauties in Spain accept bonbons from plebeian hands. It is true, most of the maskers are of the better class. Some of the costumes are very rich and expensive, of satin and velvet heavy with gold. I have seen a distinguished diplomatist in the guise of a gigantic canary-bird, hopping briskly about in the mud with bedraggled tail-feathers, shrieking well-bred sarcasms with his yellow beak.

The charm of the Madrid Carnival is this, that it is respected and believed in. The best and fairest pass the day in the Corso, and gallant young gentlemen think it worth while to dress elaborately for a few hours of harmless and spirituelle intrigue. A society that enjoys a holiday so thoroughly has something in it better than the blase cynicism of more civilized capitals. These young fellows talk like the lovers of the old romances. I have never heard prettier periods of devotion than from some gentle savage, stretched out on the front seat of a landau under the peering eyes of his lady, safe in his disguise, if not self-betrayed, pouring out his young soul in passionate praise and prayer; around them the laughter and the cries, the cracking of whips, the roll of wheels, the presence of countless thousands, and yet these two young hearts alone under the pale winter sky. The rest of the Continent has outgrown the true Carnival. It is pleasant to see this gay relic of simpler times, when youth was young. No one here is too "swell" for it. You may find a duke in the disguise of a chimney-sweep, or a butcher-boy in the dress of a Crusader. There are none so great that their dignity would suffer by a day's reckless foolery, and there are none so poor that they cannot take the price of a dinner to buy a mask and cheat their misery by mingling for a time with their betters in the wild license of the Carnival.

The winter's gayety dies hard. Ash Wednesday is a day of loud merriment and is devoted to a popular ceremony called the Burial of the Sardine. A vast throng of workingmen carry with great pomp a link of sausage to the bank of the Manzanares and inter it there with great solemnity. On the following Saturday, after three days of death, the Carnival has a resurrection, and the maddest, wildest ball of the year takes place at the opera. Then the sackcloth and ashes of Lent come down in good earnest and the town mourns over its scarlet sins. It used to be very fashionable for the genteel Christians to repair during this season of mortification to the Church of San Gines, and scourge themselves lustily in its subterranean chambers. A still more striking demonstration was for gentlemen in love to lash themselves on the sidewalks where passed the ladies of their thoughts. If the blood from the scourges sprinkled them as they sailed by, it was thought an attention no female heart could withstand. But these wholesome customs have decayed of late unbelieving years.

The Lenten piety increases with the lengthening days. It reaches its climax on Holy Thursday. On this day all Spain goes to church: it is one of the obligatory days. The more you go, the better for you; so the good people spend the whole day from dawn to dusk roaming from one church to another, and investing an Ave and a Pater-Noster in each. This fills every street of the city with the pious crowd. No carriages are permitted. A silence like that of Venice falls on the rattling capital. With three hundred thousand people in the street, the town seems still. In 1870, a free-thinking cabman dared to drive up the Calle Alcala. He was dragged from his box and beaten half to death by the chastened mourners, who yelled as they kicked and cuffed him, "Que bruto! He will wake our Jesus."

On Good Friday the gloom deepens. No colors are worn that day by the orthodox. The senoras appear on the street in funeral garb. I saw a group of fast youths come out of the jockey club, black from hat to boots, with jet studs and sleeve-buttons. The gayest and prettiest ladies sit within the church doors and beg in the holy name of charity, and earn large sums for the poor. There are hourly services in the churches, passionate sermons from all the pulpits. The streets are free from the painted haunters of the pavement. The whole people taste the luxury of a sentimental sorrow.

Yet in these heavy days it is not the Redeemer whose sufferings and death most nearly touch the hearts of the faithful. It is Santisima Maria who is worshipped most. It is the Dolorous Mother who moves them to tears of tenderness. The presiding deity of these final days of meditation is Our Lady of Solitude.

But at last the days of mourning are accomplished. The expiation for sin is finished. The grave is vanquished, death is swallowed up in victory. Man can turn from the grief that is natural to the joy that is eternal. From every steeple the bells fling out their happy clangor in glad tidings of great joy. The streets are flooded once more with eager multitudes, gay as in wedding garments. Christ has arisen! The heathen myth of the awakening of nature blends the old tradition with the new gospel. The vernal breezes sweep the skies clean and blue. Birds are pairing in the budding trees. The streams leap down from the melting snow of the hills. The brown turf takes a tint of verdure. Through the vast frame of things runs a quick shudder of teeming power. In the heart of man love and will mingle into hope. Hail to the new life and the ever-new religion! Hail to the resurrection morning!

AN HOUR WITH THE PAINTERS

As a general thing it is well to distrust a Spaniard's superlatives. He will tell you that his people are the most amiable in the world, but you will do well to carry your revolver into the interior. He will say there are no wines worth drinking but the Spanish, but you will scarcely forswear Clicquot and Yquem on the mere faith of his assertion. A distinguished general once gravely assured me that there was no literature in the world at all to be compared with the productions of the Castilian mind. All others, he said, were but pale imitations of Spanish master-work.

Now, though you may be shocked at learning such unfavorable facts of
'Shakespeare and Goethe and Hugo, you will hardly condemn them to an
Auto da fe, on the testimony even of a grandee of Spain.

But when a Spaniard assures you that the picture-gallery of Madrid is the finest in the world, you may believe him without reserve. He probably does not know what he is talking about. He may never have crossed the Pyrenees. He has no dream of the glories of Dresden, or Florence, or the Louvre. It is even possible that he has not seen the matchless collection he is boasting of. He crowns it with a sweeping superlative simply because it is Spanish. But the statement is nevertheless true.

The reason of this is found in that gigantic and overshadowing fact which seems to be an explanation of everything in Spain, — the power and the tyranny of the House of Austria. The period of the vast increase of Spanish dominion coincided with that of the meridian glory of Italian art. The conquest of Granada was finished as the divine child Raphael began to meddle with his father's brushes and pallets, and before his short life ended Charles, Burgess of Ghent, was emperor and king.

The dominions he governed and transmitted to his son embraced Spain, the Netherlands, Franche-Comte, the Milanese, Naples, and Sicily; that is to say, those regions where art in that age and the next attained its supreme development. He was also lord of the New World, whose inexhaustible mines poured into the lap of Europe a constant stream of gold. Hence came the riches and the leisure necessary to art.

Charles V., as well as his great contemporary and rival, Francis I., was a munificent protector of art. He brought from Italy and Antwerp some of the most perfect products of their immortal masters. He was the friend and patron of Titian, and when, weary of the world and its vanities, he retired to the lonely monastery of Yuste to spend in devout contemplation the evening of his days, the most precious solace of his solitude was that noble canvas of the great Venetian, where Charles and Philip are borne, in penitential guise and garb, on luminous clouds into the visible glory of the Most High.

These two great kings made a good use of their unbounded opportunities. Spain became illuminated with the glowing canvases of the incomparable Italians. The opening up of the New World beyond seas, the meteoric career of European and African conquest in which the emperor had won so much land and glory, had given an awakening shock to the intelligent youth of Spain, and sent them forth in every avenue of enterprise. This jealously patriotic race, which had remained locked up by the mountains and the seas for centuries, started suddenly out, seeking adventures over the earth. The mind of Spain seemed suddenly to have brightened and developed like that of her great king, who, in his first tourney at Valladolid, wrote with proud sluggishness *Nondum*—not yet—on his maiden shield, and a few years later in his young maturity adopted the legend of arrogant hope and promise,—*Plus Ultra*. There were seen two emigrations of the young men of Spain, eastward and westward. The latter went for gold and material conquest into the American wilds; and the former, led by the sacred love of art, to that land of beauty and wonder, then, now, and always the spiritual shrine of all peoples,—Italy.

A brilliant young army went out from Spain on this new crusade of the beautiful. From the plains of Castile and the hills of Navarre went, among others, Berruguete, Becerra, and the marvellous deaf-mute Navarrete. The luxurious city of Valentia sent Juan de Juanes and Ribalta. Luis de Vargas went out from Seville, and from Cordova the scholar, artist, and thinker, Paul of Cespedes. The schools of Rome and Venice and Florence were thronged with eager pilgrims, speaking an alien Latin and filled with a childlike wonder and appreciation.

In that stirring age the emigration was not all in one direction. Many distinguished foreigners came down to Spain, to profit by the new love of art in the Peninsula. It was Philip of Burgundy who carved, with Berruguete, those miracles of skill and patience we admire to-day in the choir of Toledo. Peter of Champagne painted at Seville the grand altar-piece that so comforted the eyes and the soul of Murillo. The wild Greek bedouin, George Theotocopouli, built the Mozarabic chapel and filled the walls of convents with his weird ghost-faces. Moor, or Moro, came from the Low Countries, and the Carducci brothers from Italy, to seek their fortunes in Madrid. Torrigiani, after breaking Michael Angelo's nose in Florence, fled to Granada, and died in a prison of the Inquisition for smashing the face of a Virgin which a grandee of Spain wanted to steal from him.

These immigrations, and the refluent tide of Spanish students from Italy, founded the various schools of Valentia, Toledo, Seville, and Madrid. Madrid soon absorbed the school of Toledo, and the attraction of Seville was too powerful for Valentia. The Andalusian school counts among its early illustrations Vargas, Roelas, the Castillos, Herrera, Pacheco, and Moya, and among its later glories Velazquez, Alonzo Cano, Zurbaran, and Murillo, last and greatest of the mighty line. The school of Madrid begins with Berruguete and Na-varrete, the Italians Caxes, Rizi, and others, who are followed by Sanchez Coello, Pantoja, Collantes. Then comes the great invader Velazquez, followed by his retainers Pareja and Carreno, and absorbs the whole life of the school. Claudio Coello makes a good fight against the rapid decadence. Luca Giordano comes rattling in from Naples with his whitewash-brush, painting a mile a minute, and classic art is ended in Spain with the brief and conscientious work of Raphael Mengs.

There is therefore little distinction of schools in Spain. Murillo, the glory of Seville, studied in Madrid, and the mighty Andalusian, Velazquez, performed his enormous life's work in the capital of Castile.

It now needs but one word to show how the Museum of Madrid became so rich in masterpieces. During the long and brilliant reigns of Charles V. and Philip II., when art had arrived at its apogee in Italy, and was just beginning its splendid career in Spain, these powerful monarchs had the lion's share of all the best work that was done in the world. There was no artist so great but he was honored by the commands of these lords of the two worlds. They thus formed in their various palaces, pleasure-houses, and cloisters a priceless collection of pictures produced in the dawn of the Spanish and the triumphant hey-day of Italian genius. Their frivolous successors lost provinces and kingdoms, honor and prestige, but they never lost their royal prerogative nor their taste for the arts. They consoled themselves for the slings and arrows of outrageous fortune by the delights of sensual life, and imagined they preserved some distant likeness to their great forerunners by encouraging and protecting Velazquez and Lope de Vega and other intellectual giants of that decaying age. So while, as the result of a vicious system of kingly and spiritual thraldom, the intellect of Spain was forced away from its legitimate channels of thought and action, under the shadow of the royal prerogative, which survived the genuine power of the older kings, art flourished and bloomed, unsuspected and unpersecuted by the coward jealousy of courtier and monk.

The palace and the convent divided the product of those marvellous days. Amid all the poverty of the failing state, it was still the king and clergy who were best able to appropriate the works of genius. This may have contributed to the decay of art. The immortal canvases passed into oblivion in the salons of palaces and the cells of monasteries. Had they been scattered over the land and seen by the people, they might have kept alive the spark that kindled their creators. But exclu-siveness is inevitably followed by barrenness. When the great race of Spanish artists ended, these matchless works were kept in the safe obscurity of palaces and religious establishments. History was working in the interests of this Museum. The pictures were held by the clenched dead hand of the Church and the throne. They could not be sold or distributed. They made the dark places luminous, patiently biding their time.

It was long enough coming, and it was a despicable hand that brought them into the light. Ferdinand VII. thought his palace would look fresher if the walls were covered with French paper, and so packed all the pictures off to the empty building on the Prado, which his grandfather had built for a museum. As soon as the glorious collection was exposed to the gaze of the world, its incontestable merit was at once recognized. Especially were the works of Velazquez, hitherto almost an unknown name in Europe, admired and appreciated. Ferdinand, finding he had done a clever thing unawares, began to put on airs and poser for a patron of art. The gallery was still further immensely enriched on the exclaustra-tion of the monasteries, by the hidden treasures of the Escorial, and other spoils of mortmain. And now, as a collection of masterpieces, it has no equal in the world.

A few figures will prove this. It contains more than two thousand pictures already catalogued,—all of them worth a place on the walls. Among these there are ten by Raphael, forty-three by Titian, thirty-four by Tintoret, twenty-five by Paul Veronese. Rubens has the enormous contingent of sixty-four. Of Teniers, whose works are sold for fabulous sums for the square inch, this extraordinary museum possesses no less than sixty finished pictures,—the Louvre considers itself rich with fourteen. So much for a few of the foreigners. Among the Spaniards the three greatest names could alone fill a gallery. There are sixty-five Velazquez, forty-six Murillos, and fifty-eight Riberas. Compare these figures with those of any other gallery in existence, and you will at once recognize the hopeless superiority of this collection. It is not only the greatest collection in the world, but the greatest that can ever be made until this is broken up.

But with all this mass of wealth it is not a complete, nor, properly speaking, a representative museum. You cannot trace upon its walls the slow, groping progress of art towards perfection. It contains few of what the book-lovers call *incunabula*. Spanish art sprang out full-armed from the mature brain of Rome. Juan de Juanes carne back from Italy a great artist. The schools of Spain were budded on a full-bearing tree. Charles and Philip bought masterpieces, and cared Jittle for the crude efforts of the awkward pencils of the necessary men who came before Raphael. There is not a Perugino in Madrid. There is nothing Byzantine, no trace of Renaissance; nothing of the patient work of the early Flemings, — the art of Flanders comes blazing in with the full splendor of Rubens and Van Dyck. And even among the masters, the representation is most unequal. Among the wilderness of Titians and Tintorets you find but two Domenichinos and two Correg-gios. Even in Spanish art the gallery is far from complete. There is almost nothing of such genuine painters as Zurbaran and Herrera.

But recognizing all this, there is, in this glorious temple, enough to fill the least enthusiastic lover of art with delight and adoration for weeks and months together. If one knew he was to be blind in a year, like the young musician in Auerbach's exquisite romance, I know of no place in the world where he could garner up so precious a store of memories for the days of darkness, memories that would haunt the soul with so divine a light of consolation, as in that graceful Palace of the Prado.

It would be a hopeless task to attempt to review with any detail the gems of this collection. My memory is filled with the countless canvases that adorn the ten great halls. If I refer to my notebook I am equally discouraged by the number I have marked for special notice. The masterpieces are simply innumerable. I will say a word of each room, and so give up the unequal contest.

As you enter the Museum from the north, you are in a wide sturdy-columned vestibule, hung with splashy pictures of Luca Giordano. To your right is the room devoted to the Spanish school; to the left, the Italian. In front is the grand gallery where the greatest works of both schools are collected. In the Spanish saloon there is an indefinable air of severity and gloom. It is less perfectly lighted than some others, and there is something forbidding in the general tone of the room. There are prim portraits of queens and princes, monks in contemplation, and holy people in antres vast and deserts idle. Most visitors come in from a sense of duty, look hurriedly about, and go out with a conscience at ease; in fact, there is a dim suggestion of the fagot and the rack about many of the Spanish masters. At one end of this gallery the Prometheus of Ribera agonizes chained to his rock. His gigantic limbs are flung about in the fury of immortal pain. A vulture, almost lost in the blackness of the shadows, is tugging at his vitals. His brow is convulsed with the pride and anguish of a demigod. It is a picture of horrible power. Opposite hangs one of the few Zurbarans of the gallery,—also a gloomy and terrible work. A monk kneels in shadows which, by the masterly chiaroscuro of this ascetic artist, are made to look darker than blackness. Before him in a luminous nimbus that burns its way through the dark, is the image of the crucified Saviour, head downwards. So remarkable is the vigor of the drawing and the power of light in this picture that you can imagine you see the resplendent crucifix suddenly thrust into the shadow by the strong hands of invisible spirits, and swayed for a moment only before the dazzled eyes of the ecstatic solitary.

But after you have made friends with this room it will put off its forbidding aspect, and you will find it hath a stern look but a gentle heart. It has two lovely little landscapes by Murillo, showing how universal was that wholesome genius. Also one of the largest landscapes of Velazquez, which, when you stand near it, seems a confused mass of brown daubs, but stepping back a few yards becomes a most perfect view of the entrance to a royal park. The wide gate swings on its pivot before your eyes. A court cortege moves in,—the long, dark alley stretches off for miles directly in front, without any trick of lines or curves; the artist has painted the shaded air. To the left a patch of still water reflects the dark wood, and above there is a distant and tranquil sky. Had Velazquez not done such vastly greater things, his few landscapes would alone have won him fame enough. He has in this room a large number of royal portraits,—one especially worth attention, of Philip III. The scene is by the shore,— a cool foreground of sandy beach,—a blue-gray stretch of rippled water, and beyond, a low promontory between the curling waves and the cirrus clouds. The king mounts a magnificent gray horse, with a mane and tail like the broken rush of a cascade. The keeping is wonderful; a fresh sea breeze blows out of the canvas. A brilliant bit of color is thrown into the red, gold-fringed scarf of the horseman, fluttering backward over his shoulder. Yet the face of the king is, as it should be, the principal point of the picture,—the small-eyed, heavy-mouthed, red-lipped, fair, self-satisfied face of these Austrian despots. It is a handsomer face than most of Velazquez, as it was probably painted from memory and lenient tradition. For Philip III. was gathered to his fathers in the Escorial before Velazquez came up from Andalusia to seek his fortune at the court. The first work he did in Madrid was to paint the portrait of the king, which so pleased his majesty that he had it repeated *ad nauseam.* You see him served up in every form in this gallery,—on foot, on horseback, in full armor, in a shooting-jacket, at picnics, and actually on his knees at his prayers! We wonder if Velazquez ever grew tired of that vacant face with its contented smirk, or if in that loyal age the smile of royalty was not always the sunshine of the court?

There is a most instructive study of faces in the portraits of the Austrian line. First comes Charles V., the First of Spain, painted by Titian at Augsburg, on horseback, in the armor he wore at Muhlberg, his long lance in rest, his visor up over the eager, powerful face,—the eye and beak of an eagle, the jaw of a bull-dog, the face of a born ruler, a man of prey. And yet in the converging lines about the eyes, in the premature gray hair, in the nervous, irritable lips, you can see the promise of early decay, of an age that will be the spoil of superstition and bigotry. It is the face of a man who could make himself emperor and hermit. In his son, Philip II., the soldier dies out and the bigot is intensified. In the fine portrait by Pantoja, of Philip in his age, there is scarcely any trace of the fresh, fair youth that Titian painted as Adonis. It is the face of a living corpse; of a ghastly pallor, heightened by the dull black of his mourning suit, where all passion and feeling have died out of the livid lips and the icy eyes. Beside him hangs the portrait of his rickety, feebly passionate son, the unfortunate Don Carlos. The forehead of the young prince is narrow and ill-formed; the Austrian chin is exaggerated one degree more; he looks a picture of fitful impulse. His brother, Philip III., we have just seen, fair and inane,—a monster of cruelty, who burned Jews and banished Moors, not from malice, but purely from vacuity of spirit; his head broadens like a pine-apple from the blond crest to the plump jowls. Every one knows the head of Philip

IV.,—he was fortunate in being the friend of Velazquez,—the high, narrow brow, the long, weak face, the yellow, curled mustache, the thick, red lips, and the ever lengthening Hapsburg chin. But the line of Austria ends with the utmost limit of caricature in the face of Charles the Bewitched! Carreno has given us an admirable portrait of this unfortunate,—the forehead caved in like the hat of a drunkard, the red-lidded eyes staring vacantly, a long, thin nose absurd as a Carnival disguise, an enormous mouth which he could not shut, the under-jaw projected so prodigiously,—a face incapable of any emotion but fear. And yet in gazing at this idiotic mask you are reminded of another face you have somewhere seen, and are startled to remember it is the resolute face of the warrior and statesman, the king of men, the Kaiser Karl. Yes, this pitiable being was the descendant of the great emperor, and for that sufficient reason, although he was an impotent and shivering idiot, although he could not sleep without a friar in his bed to keep the devils away, for thirty-five years this scarecrow ruled over Spain, and dying made a will whose accomplishment bathed the Peninsula in blood. It must be confessed this institution of monarchy is a luxury that must be paid for.

We did not intend to talk of politics in this room, but that line of royal effigies was too tempting. Before we go, let us look at a beautiful Magdalen in penitence, by an unknown artist of the school of Murillo. She stands near the entrance of her cave, in a listening attitude. The bright out-of-door light falls on her bare shoulder and gives the faintest touch of gold to her dishevelled brown hair. She casts her eyes upward, the large melting eyes of Andalusia; a chastened sorrow, through which a trembling hope is shining, softens the somewhat worldly beauty of her exquisite and sensitive face. Through the mouth of the cave we catch a glimpse of sunny mountain solitude, and in the rosy air that always travels with Spanish angels a band of celestial serenaders is playing. It is a charming composition, without any depth of sentiment or especial mastery of treatment, but evidently painted by a clever artist in his youth, and this Magdalen is the portrait of the lady of his dreams. None of Murillo's pupils but Tobar could have painted it, and the manner is precisely the same as that of his Divina Pastora.

Across the hall is the gallery consecrated to Italian artists. There are not many pictures of the first rank here. They have been reserved for the great central gallery, where we are going. But while here, we must notice especially two glorious works of Tintoret, — the same subject differently treated, — the Death of Holofernes. Both are placed higher than they should be, considering their incontestable merit. A full light is needed to do justice to that magnificence of color which is the pride of Venice. There are two remarkable pictures of Giordano, — one in the Roman style, which would not be unworthy of the great Sanzio himself, a Holy Family, drawn and colored with that scrupulous correctness which seems so impossible in the ordinary products of this Protean genius; and just opposite, an apotheosis of Rubens, surrounded by his usual "properties" of fat angels and genii, which could be readily sold anywhere as a specimen of the estimate which the unabashed Fleming placed upon himself. It is marvellous that any man should so master the habit and the thought of two artists so widely apart as Raphael and Rubens, as to produce just such pictures as they would have painted upon the same themes. The halls and dark corridors of the Museum are filled with Giordano's canvases. In less than ten years' residence in Spain he covered the walls of dozens of churches and palaces with his fatally facile work. There are more than three hundred pictures recorded as executed by him in that time. They are far from being without merit. There is a singular slap-dash vigor about his drawing. His coloring, except when he is imitating some earlier master, is usually thin and poor. It is difficult to repress an emotion of regret in looking at his laborious yet useless life. With great talents, with indefatigable industry, he deluged Europe with paintings that no one cares for, and passed into history simply as Luca Fa Presto, — Luke Work-Fast.

It is not by mere activity that great things are done in art. In the great gallery we now enter we see the deathless work of the men who wrought in faith. This is the grandest room in Christendom. It is about three hundred and fifty feet long and thirty-five broad and high. It is beautifully lighted from above. Its great length is broken here and there by vases and statues, so placed between doors as nowhere to embarrass the view. The northern half of the gallery is Spanish, and the southern half Italian. Halfway down, a door to the left opens into an oval chamber, devoted to an eclectic set of masterpieces of every school and age. The gallery ends in a circular room of French and German pictures, on either side of which there are two great halls of Dutch and Flemish. On the ground floor there are some hundreds more Flemish and a hall of sculpture.

The first pictures you see to your left are by the early masters of Spain,—Morales, called in Spain the Divine, whose works are now extremely rare, the Museum possessing only three or four, long, fleshless faces and stiff figures of Christs and Marys,—and Juan de Juanes, the founder of the Valentian school, who brought back from Italy the lessons of Raphael's studio, that firmness of design and brilliancy of color, and whose genuine merit has survived all vicissitudes of changing taste. He has here a superb Last Supper and a spirited series of pictures illustrating the martyrdom of Stephen. There is perhaps a little too much elaboration of detail, even for the Romans. Stephen's robes are unnecessarily new, and the ground where he is stoned is profusely covered with convenient round missiles the size of Vienna rolls, so exactly suited to the purpose that it looks as if Providence sided with the persecutors. But what a wonderful variety and truth in the faces and the attitudes of the groups! What mastery of drawing, and what honest integrity of color after all these ages! It is reported of Juanes that he always confessed and prayed before venturing to take up his pencils to touch the features of the saints and Saviours that shine on his canvas. His conscientious fervor has its reward.

Across the room are the Murillos. Hung together are two pictures, not of large dimensions, but of exquisite perfection, which will serve as fair illustrations of the work of his youth and his age; the frio and the vaporoso manner. In the former manner is this charming picture of Rebecca at the Well; a graceful composition, correct and somewhat severe drawing, the greatest sharpness and clearness of outline. In the Martyrdom of St. Andrew the drawing and the composition are no less absolutely perfect, but there hangs over the whole picture a luminous haze of strangeness and mystery. A light that never was on sea or land bathes the distant hills and battlements, touches the spears of the legionaries, and shines in full glory on the ecstatic face of the aged saint. It does not seem a part of the scene. You see the picture through it. A step further on there is a

Holy Family, which seems to me the ultimate effort of the early manner. A Jewish carpenter holds his fair-haired child between his knees. The urchin holds up a bird to attract the attention of a little white dog on the floor. The mother, a dark-haired peasant woman, looks on the scene with quiet amusement. The picture is absolutely perfect in detail. It seems to be the *consigne* among critics to say it lacks "style." They say it is a family scene in Judaea, *voila tout.* Of course, and it is that very truth and nature that makes this picture so fascinating. The Word was made flesh, and not a phosphorescent apparition; and Murillo knew what he was about when he painted this view of the interior of St. Joseph's shop. What absurd presumption to accuse this great thinker of a deficiency of ideality, in face of these two glorious Marys of the Conception that fill the room with light and majesty! They hang side by side, so alike and yet so distinct in character. One is a woman in knowledge and a goddess of purity; the other, absolute innocence, startled by the stupendous revelation and exalted by the vaguely comprehended glory of the future. It is before this picture that the visitor always lingers longest. The face is the purest expression of girlish loveliness possible to art. The Virgin floats upborne by rosy clouds, flocks of pink cherubs flutter at her feet waving palm-branches. The golden air is thick with suggestions of dim celestial faces, but nothing mars the imposing solitude of the Queen of Heaven, shrined alone, throned in the luminous azure. Surely no man ever understood or interpreted like this grand Andalusian the power that the worship of woman exerts on the religions of the world. All the passionate love that has been poured out in all the ages at the feet of Ashtaroth and Artemis and Aphrodite and Freya found visible form and color at last on that immortal canvas where, with his fervor of religion and the full strength of his virile devotion to beauty, he created, for the adoration of those who should follow him, this type of the perfect Feminine, —

"Thee! standing loveliest in the open heaven! Ave Maria! only
Heaven and
Thee!"

There are some dozens more of Murillo here almost equally remarkable, but I cannot stop to make an unmeaning catalogue of them. There is a charming Gypsy Fortune-teller, whose wheedling voice and smile were caught and fixed in some happy moment in Seville; an Adoration of the Shepherds, wonderful in its happy combination of rigid truth with the warmest glow of poetry; two Annunciations, rich with the radiance that streams through the rent veil of the innermost heaven, — lights painted boldly upon lights, the White Dove sailing out of the dazzling background of celestial effulgence, — a miracle and mystery of theology repeated by a miracle and mystery of art.

Even when you have exhausted the Murillos of the Museum you have not reached his highest achievements in color and design. You will find these in the Academy of San Fernando, — the Dream of the Roman Gentleman, and the Founding of the Church of St. Mary the Greater; and the powerful composition of St. Elizabeth of Hungary, in her hospital work. In the first, a noble Roman and his wife have suddenly fallen asleep in their chairs in an elegant apartment. Their slumber is painted with curious felicity, — you lower your voice for fear of waking them. On the left of the picture is their dream: the Virgin comes in a halo of golden clouds and designates the spot where her church is to be built. In the next picture the happy couple kneel before the pope and expose their high commission, and outside a brilliant procession moves to the ceremony of the laying of the corner-stone. The St. Elizabeth is a triumph of genius over a most terribly repulsive subject. The wounds and sores of the beggars are painted with unshrinking fidelity, but every vulgar detail is redeemed by the beauty and majesty of the whole. I think in these pictures of Murillo the last word of Spanish art was reached. There was no further progress possible in life, even for him. "Other heights in other lives, God willing."

Returning to the Museum and to Velazquez, we find ourselves in front of his greatest historical work, the Surrender of Breda. This is probably the most utterly unaffected historical painting in existence. There is positively no stage business about it. On the right is the Spanish staff, on the left the deputation of the vanquished Flemings. In the centre the great Spinola accepts the keys of the city from the governor; his attitude and face are full of dignity softened by generous and affable grace. He lays his hand upon the shoulder of the Flemish general, and you can see he is paying him some chivalrous compliment on the gallant fight he has lost. If your eyes wander through the open space between the two escorts, you see a wonderful widespread landscape in the Netherlands, which would form a fine picture if the figures all were gone. Opposite this great work is another which artists consider greater,—Las Meninas. When Luca Giordano came from Italy he inquired for this picture, and said on seeing it, "This is the theology of painting." If our theology were what it should be, and cannot be, absolute and unquestionable truth, Luca the Quick-worker would have been right. Velazquez was painting the portrait of a stupid little infanta when the idea came to him of perpetuating the scene just as it was. We know how we have wished to be sure of the exact accessories of past events. The modern rage for theatrical local color is an illustration of this desire. The great artist, who must have honored his art, determined to give to future ages an exact picture of one instant of his glorious life. It is not too much to say he has done this. He stands before his easel, his pencils in his hand. The little princess is stiffly posing in the centre. Her little maids are grouped about her. Two hideous dwarfs on the right are teasing a noble dog who is too drowsy and magnanimous to growl. In the background at the end of a long gallery a gentleman is opening a door to the garden. The presence of royalty is indicated by the reflection of the faces of the king and queen in a small mirror, where you would expect to see your own. The longer you look upon this marvellous painting, the less possible does it seem that it is merely the placing of color on canvas which causes this perfect illusion. It does not seem possible that you are looking at a plane surface. There is a stratum of air before, behind, and beside these figures. You could walk on that floor and see how the artist is getting on with the portrait. There is space and light in this picture, as in any room. Every object is detached, as in the common miracle of the stereoscope. If art consist in making a fleeting moment immortal, if the True is a higher ideal than the Beautiful, then it will be hard to find a greater painting than this. It is utterly without beauty; its tone is a cold olive green-gray; there is not one redeeming grace or charm about it except the noble figure of Velazquez himself,—yet in its austere fidelity to truth it stands incomparable in the world. It gained Velazquez his greatest triumph. You see on his breast a sprawling red cross, painted evidently by an unskilful hand. This was the gracious answer made by Philip IV.

when the artist asked him if anything was wanting to the picture. This decoration, daubed by the royal hand, was the accolade of the knighthood of Santiago,—an honor beyond the dreams of an artist of that day. It may be considered the highest compliment ever paid to a painter, except the one paid by Courbet to himself, when he refused to be decorated by the Man of December.

Among Velazquez's most admirable studies of life is his picture of the Borrachos. A group of rustic roysterers are admitting a neophyte into the drunken *confrerie*. He kneels to receive a crown of ivy from the hands of the king of the revel. A group of older tipplers are filling their cups, or eyeing their brimming glasses, with tipsy, mock-serious glances. There has never been a chapter written which so clearly shows the drunkard's nature as this vulgar anacreontic. A thousand men have painted drunken frolics, but never one with such distinct spiritual insight as this. To me the finest product of Jordaens' genius is his Bohnen Koenig in the Belvedere, but there you see only the incidents of the mad revel; every one is shouting or singing or weeping with maudlin glee or tears. But in this scene of the Borrachos there is nothing scenic or forced. These topers have come together to drink, for the love of the wine,—the fun is secondary. This wonderful reserve of Velazquez is clearly seen in his conception of the king of the rouse. He is a young man, with a heavy, dull, somewhat serious face, fat rather than bloated, rather pale than flushed. He is naked to the waist to show the plump white arms and shoulders and the satiny skin of the voluptuary; one of those men whose heads and whose stomachs are too loyal ever to give them *Katzenjammer* or remorse. The others are of the commoner type of haunters of wine-shops,—with red eyes and coarse hides and grizzled matted hair,—but every man of them inexorably true, and a predestined sot.

We must break away from Velazquez, passing by his marvellous portraits of kings and dwarfs, saints and poodles,—among whom there is a dwarf of two centuries ago, who is too like Tom Thumb to serve for his twin brother,—and a portrait of Aesop, which is a flash of intuition, an epitome of all the fables. Before leaving the Spaniards we must look at the most pleasing of all Ribera's works,—the Ladder-Dream of Jacob. The patriarch lies stretched on the open plain in the deep sleep of the weary. To the right in a broad shaft of cloudy gold the angels are ascending and descending. The picture is remarkable for its mingling the merits of Ribera's first and second manner. It is a Caravaggio in its strength and breadth of light and shade, and a Correggio in its delicacy of sentiment and refined beauty of coloring. He was not often so fortunate in his Parmese efforts. They are usually marked by a timidity and an attempt at prettiness inconceivable in the haughty and impulsive master of the Neapolitan school.

Of the three great Spaniards, Ribera is the least sympathetic. He often displays a tumultuous power and energy to which his calmer rivals are strangers. But you miss in him that steady devotion to truth which distinguishes Velazquez, and that spiritual lift which ennobles Murillo. The difference, I conceive, lies in the moral character of the three. Ribera was a great artist, and the others were noble men. Ribera passed a youth of struggle and hunger and toil among the artists of Rome,—a stranger and penniless in the magnificent city,—picking up crusts in the street and sketching on quiet curbstones, with no friend, and no name but that of Spagnoletto,—the little Spaniard. Suddenly rising to fame, he broke loose from his Roman associations and fled to Naples, where he soon became the wealthiest and the most arrogant artist of his time. He held continually at his orders a faction of *bravi* who drove from Naples, with threats and insults and violence, every artist of eminence who dared visit the city. Car-racci and Guido only saved their lives by flight, and the blameless and gifted Domenichino, it is said, was foully murdered by his order. It is not to such a heart as this that is given the ineffable raptures of Murillo or the positive revelations of Velazquez. These great souls were above cruelty or jealousy. Velazquez never knew the storms of adversity. Safely anchored in the royal favor, he passed his uneventful life in the calm of his beloved work. But his hand and home were always open to the struggling artists of Spain. He was the benefactor of Alonzo Cano; and when Murillo came up to Madrid, weary and footsore with his long tramp from Andalusia, sustained by an innate consciousness of power, all on fire with a picture of Van Dyck he had seen in Seville, the rich and honored painter of the court received with generous kindness the shabby young wanderer, clothed him, and taught him, and watched with noble delight the first flights of the young eagle whose strong wing was so soon to cleave the empyrean. And when Murillo went back to Seville he paid his debt by doing as much for others. These magnanimous hearts were fit company for the saints they drew.

We have lingered so long with the native artists we shall have little to say of the rest. There are ten fine Raphaels, but it is needless to speak of them. They have been endlessly reproduced. Raphael is known and judged by the world. After some centuries of discussion the scorners and the critics are dumb. All men have learned the habit of Albani, who, in a frivolous and unappreciative age, always uncovered his head at the name of Raphael Sanzio. We look at his precious work with a mingled feeling of gratitude for what we have, and of rebellious wonder that lives like his and Shelley's should be extinguished in their glorious dawn, while kings and country gentlemen live a hundred years. What boundless possibilities of bright achievement these two divine youths owed us in the forty years more they should have lived! Raphael's greatest pictures in Madrid are the Spasimo di Sicilia, and the Holy Family, called La Perla. The former has a singular history. It was painted for a convent in Palermo, shipwrecked on the way, and thrown ashore on the gulf of Genoa. It was again sent to Sicily, brought to Spain by the Viceroy of Naples, stolen by Napoleon, and in Paris was subjected to a brilliantly successful operation for transferring the layer of paint from the worm-eaten wood to canvas. It came back to Spain with other stolen goods from the Louvre. La Perla was bought by Philip IV. at the sale of Charles I.'s effects after his decapitation. Philip was fond of Charles, but could not resist the temptation to profit by his death. This picture was the richest of the booty. It is, of all the faces of the Virgin extant, the most perfectly beautiful and one of the least spiritual.

There is another fine Madonna, commonly called La Virgen del Pez, from a fish which young Tobit holds in his hand. It is rather tawny in color, as if it had been painted on a pine board and the wood had asserted itself from below. It is a charming picture, with all the great Roman's inevitable perfection of design; but it is incomprehensible that critics, M. Viardot among them, should call it the first in rank of Raphael's Virgins in Glory. There are none which can dispute that title with Our Lady of San Sisto, unearthly and supernatural in beauty and majesty.

The school of Florence is represented by a charming Mona Lisa of Leonardo da Vinci, almost identical with that of the Louvre; and six admirable pictures of Andrea del Sarto. But the one which most attracts and holds all those who regard the Faultless Painter with sympathy, and who admiring his genius regret his errors, is a portrait of his wife Lucrezia Fede, whose name, a French writer has said, is a double epigram. It was this capricious and wilful beauty who made poor Andrea break his word and embezzle the money King Francis had given him to spend for works of art. Yet this dangerous face is his best excuse,—the face of a man-snarer, subtle and passionate and cruel in its blind selfishness, and yet so beautiful that any man might yield to it against the cry of his own warning conscience. Browning must have seen it before he wrote, in his pathetic poem,—

"Let my hands frame your face in your hair's gold,
You beautiful Lucrezia, that are mine!"

Nowhere, away from the Adriatic, is the Venetian school so richly represented as in Madrid. Charles and Philip were the most munificent friends and patrons of Titian, and the Royal Museum counts among its treasures in consequence the enormous number of forty-three pictures by the wonderful centenarian. Among these are two upon which he set great value,—a Last Supper, which has unfortunately mouldered to ruin in the humid refectory of the Escorial, equal in merit and destiny with that of Leonardo; and the Gloria, or apotheosis of the imperial family, which, after the death of Charles, was brought from Yuste to the Escorial, and thence came to swell the treasures of the Museum. It is a grand and masterly work. The vigorous genius of Titian has grappled with the essential difficulties of a subject that trembles on the balance of ridiculous and sublime, and has come out triumphant. The Father and the Son sit on high. The Operating Spirit hovers above them. The Virgin in robes of azure stands in the blaze of the Presence. The celestial army is ranged around. Below, a little lower than the angels, are Charles and Philip with their wives, on their knees, with white cowls and clasped hands,—Charles in his premature age, with worn face and grizzled beard; and Philip in his youth of unwholesome fairness, with red lips and pink eyelids, such as Titian painted him in the Adonis. The foreground is filled with prophets and saints of the first dignity, and a kneeling woman, whose face is not visible, but whose attitude and drapery are drawn with the sinuous and undulating grace of that hand which could not fail. Every figure is turned to the enthroned Deity, touched with ineffable light. The artist has painted heaven, and is not absurd. In that age of substantial faith such achievements were possible.

There are two Venuses by Titian very like that of Dresden, but the heads have not the same dignity; and a Danae which is a replica of the Vienna one. His Salome bearing the Head of John the Baptist is one of the finest impersonations of the pride of life conceivable. So unapproachable are the soft lights and tones on the perfect arms and shoulders of the full-bodied maiden, that Tintoret one day exclaimed in despair before it, "That fellow paints with ground flesh."

This gallery possesses one of the last works of Titian,—the Battle of Lepanto, which was fought when the artist was ninety-four years of age. It is a courtly allegory,—King Philip holds his little son in his arms, a courier angel brings the news of victory, and to the infant a palm-branch and the scroll *Majora tibi*. Outside you see the smoke and flash of a naval battle, and a malignant and tur-baned Turk lies bound on the floor. It would seem incredible that this enormous canvas should have been executed at such an age, did we not know that when the pest cut the mighty master off in his hundredth year he was busily at work upon a Descent from the Cross, which Palma the Elder finished on his knees and dedicated to God: Quod Titianus inchoatum reliquit Palma reverenter absolvit Deoque dicavit opus.

The vast representation of Titian rather injures Veronese and Tintoret. Opposite the Gloria of Yuste hangs the sketch of that stupendous Paradise of Tintoret, which we see in the Palace of the Doges,—the biggest picture ever painted by mortal, thirty feet high and seventy-four long.

The sketch was secured by Velazquez in his tour through Italy. The most charming picture of Veronese is a Venus and Adonis, which is finer than that of Titian,—a classic and most exquisite idyl of love and sleep, cool shadow and golden-sifted sunshine. His most considerable work in the gallery is a Christ teaching the Doctors, magnificent in arrangement, severely correct in drawing, and of a most vivid and dramatic interest.

We pass through a circular vaulted chamber to reach the Flemish rooms. There is a choice though scanty collection of the German and French schools. Albert Durer has an Adam and Eve, and a priceless portrait of himself as perfectly preserved as if it were painted yesterday. He wears a curious and picturesque costume,—striped black-and-white,—a graceful tasselled cap of the same. The picture is sufficiently like the statue at Nuremberg; a long South-German face, blue-eyed and thin, fair-whiskered, with that expression of quiet confidence you would expect in the man who said one day, with admirable candor, when people were praising a picture of his, "It could not be better done." In this circular room are four great Claudes, two of which, Sunrise and Sunset, otherwise called the Embarcation of Sta. Paula, and Tobit and the Angel, are in his best and richest manner. It is inconceivable to us, who graduate men by a high-school standard, that these refined and most elegant works could have been produced by a man so imperfectly educated as Claude Lorrain.

There remain the pictures of the Dutch and the Flemings. It is due to the causes we have mentioned in the beginning that neither in Antwerp nor Dresden nor Paris is there such wealth and profusion of the Netherlands art as in this mountain-guarded corner of Western Europe. I shall have but a word to say of these three vast rooms, for Rubens and Van Dyck and Teniers are known to every one. The first has here a representation so complete that if Europe were sunk by a cataclysm from the Baltic to the Pyrenees every essential characteristic of the great Fleming could still be studied in this gallery. With the exception of his Descent from the Cross in the Cathedral at Antwerp, painted in a moment of full inspiration that never comes twice in a life, everything he has done elsewhere may be matched in Madrid. His largest picture here is an Adoration of the Kings, an overpowering exhibition of wasteful luxuriance of color and *fougue* of composition. To the left the Virgin stands leaning with queenly majesty over the effulgent Child. From this point the light flashes out over the kneeling magi, the gorgeously robed attendants, the prodigality of velvet and jewels and gold, to fade into the lovely clear-obscure of a starry night peopled with dim camels and cattle. On the extreme right is a most graceful and gallant portrait of the artist on horseback. We have another fine self-portraiture in the Garden of Love,—a group of lords and ladies in a delicious pleasance where the greatest seigneur is Peter Paul Rubens and the finest lady is Helen Forman. These true artists had to paint for money so many ignoble faces that they could not be blamed for taking their revenge in painting sometimes their own noble heads. Van Dyck never drew a profile so faultless in manly beauty as his own which we see on the same canvas with that of his friend the Earl of Bristol. Look at the two faces side by side, and say whether God or the king can make the better nobleman.

Among those mythological subjects in which Rubens delighted, the best here are his Perseus and Andromeda, where the young hero comes gloriously in a brand-new suit of Milanese armor, while the lovely princess, in a costume that never grows old-fashioned, consisting of sunshine and golden hair, awaits him and deliverance in beautiful resignation; a Judgment of Paris, the Three Graces,—both prodigies of his strawberries-and-cream color; and a curious suckling of Hercules, which is the prototype or adumbration of the ecstatic vision of St. Bernard. He has also a copy of Titian's Adam and Eve, in an out-of-the-way place downstairs, which should be hung beside the original, to show the difference of handling of the two master colorists.

Especially happy is this Museum in its Van Dycks. Besides those incomparable portraits of Lady Oxford, of Liberti the Organist of Antwerp, and others better than the best of any other man, there are a few large and elaborate compositions such as I have never seen elsewhere. The principal one is the Capture of Christ by Night in the Garden of Gethsemane, which has all the strength of Rubens, with a more refined study of attitudes and a greater delicacy of tone and touch. Another is the Crowning with Thorns,—although of less dimensions, of profound significance in expression, and a flowing and marrowy softness of execution. You cannot survey the work of Van Dyck in this collection, so full of deep suggestion, showing an intellect so vivid and so refined, a mastery of processes so thorough and so intelligent, without the old wonder of what he would have done in that ripe age when Titian and Murillo and Shakespeare wrought their best and fullest, and the old regret for the dead,—as Edgar Poe sings, the doubly dead in that they died so young. We are tempted to lift the veil that hides the unknown, at least with the furtive hand of conjecture; to imagine a field of unquenched activity where the early dead, free from the clogs and trammels of the lower world, may follow out the impulses of their diviner nature,—where Andrea has no wife, and Raphael and Van Dyck no disease,—where Keats and Shelley have all eternity for their lofty rhyme,—where Ellsworth and Koerner and the Lowell boys can turn their alert and athletic intelligence to something better than war.

A CASTLE IN THE AIR

I have sometimes thought that a symptom of the decay of true kinghood in modern times is the love of monarchs for solitude. In the early days when monarchy was a real power to answer a real want, the king had no need to hide himself. He was the strongest, the most knowing, the most cunning. He moved among men their acknowledged chief. He guided and controlled them. He never lost his dignity by daily use. He could steal a horse like Diomede, he could mend his own breeches like Dagobert, and never tarnish the lustre of the crown by it. But in later times the throne has become an anachronism. The wearer of a crown has done nothing to gain it but give himself the trouble to be born. He has no claim to the reverence or respect of men. Yet he insists upon it, and receives some show of it. His life is mainly passed in keeping up this battle for a lost dignity and worship. He is given up to shams and ceremonies.

To a life like this there is something embarrassing in the movement and activity of a great city. The king cannot join in it without a loss of prestige. Being outside of it, he is vexed and humiliated by it. The empty forms become nauseous in the midst of this honest and wholesome reality of out-of-doors.

Hence the necessity of these quiet retreats in the forests, in the water-guarded islands, in the cloud-girdled mountains. Here the world is not seen or heard. Here the king may live with such approach to nature as his false and deformed education will allow. He is surrounded by nothing but the world of servants and courtiers, and it requires little effort of the imagination to consider himself chief and lord.

It was this spirit which in the decaying ripeness of the Bourbon dynasty drove the Louis from Paris to Versailles and from Versailles to Marly. Millions were wasted to build the vast monument of royal fatuity, and when it was done the Grand Monarque found it necessary to fly from time to time to the sham solitude and mock retirement he had built an hour away.

When Philip V. came down from France to his splendid exile on the throne of Spain, he soon wearied of the interminable ceremonies of the Cas-tilian court, and finding one day, while hunting, a pleasant farm on the territory of the Segovian monks, flourishing in a wrinkle of the Guadarrama Mountains, he bought it, and reared the Palace of La Granja. It is only kings who can build their castles in the air of palpable stones and mortar. This lordly pleasure-house stands four thousand feet above the sea level. On this commanding height, in this savage Alpine loneliness, in the midst of a scenery once wildly beautiful, but now shorn and shaven into a smug likeness of a French garden, Philip passed all the later years of his gloomy and inglorious life.

It has been ever since a most tempting summer-house to all the Bourbons. When the sun is calcining the plains of Castile, and the streets of Madrid are white with the hot light of midsummer, this palace in the clouds is as cool and shadowy as spring twilights. And besides, as all public business is transacted in Madrid, and La Granja is a day's journey away, it is too much trouble to send a courier every day for the royal signature,—or, rather, rubric, for royalty in Spain is above handwriting, and gives its majestic approval with a flourish of the pen,—so that everything waits a week or so, and much business goes finally undone; and this is the highest triumph of Spanish industry and skill.

We had some formal business with the court of the regent, and were not sorry to learn that his highness would not return to the capital for some weeks, and that consequently, following the precedent of a certain prophet, we must go to the mountain.

We found at the Estacion del Norte the state railway carriage of her late majesty,—a brilliant creation of yellow satin and profuse gilding, a bovidoir on wheels,—not too full of a distinguished company. Some of the leading men of New Spain, one or two ministers, were there, and we passed a pleasant two hours on the road in that most seductive of all human occupations,—talking politics.

It is remarkable that whenever a nation is remodelling its internal structure, the subject most generally discussed is the constitutional system of the United States. The republicans usually adopt it solid. The monarchists study it with a jealous interest. I fell into conversation with Senor — — —, one of the best minds in Spain, an enlightened though conservative statesman. He said: "It is hard for Europe to adopt a settled belief about you. America is a land of wonders, of contradictions. One party calls your system freedom, another anarchy. In all legislative assemblies of Europe, republicans and absolutists alike draw arguments from America. But what cannot be denied are the effects, the results. These are evident, something vast and grandiose, a life and movement to which the Old World is stranger." He afterwards referred with great interest to the imaginary imperialist movement in America, and raised his eyebrows in polite incredulity when I assured him there was as much danger of Spain becoming Mohammedan as of America becoming imperialist.

We stopped at the little station of Villalba, in the midst of the wide brown table-land that stretches from Madrid to the Escorial. At Villalba we found the inevitable swarm of beggars, who always know by the sure instinct of wretchedness where a harvest of cuartos is to be achieved. I have often passed Villalba and have seen nothing but the station-master and the water-vender. But to-day, because there were a half dozen excellencies on the train, the entire mendicant force of the district was on parade. They could not have known these gentlemen were coming; they must have scented pennies in the air.

Awaiting us at the rear of the station were three enormous lumbering diligences, each furnished with nine superb mules, — four pairs and a leader. They were loaded with gaudy trappings, and their shiny coats, and backs shorn into graceful arabesques, showed that they did not belong to the working-classes, but enjoyed the gentlemanly leisure of official station. The drivers wore a smart postilion uniform and the royal crown on their caps.

We threw some handfuls of copper and bronze among the picturesque mendicants. They gathered them up with grave Castilian decorum, and said, "God will repay your graces." The postilions cracked their whips, the mules shook their bells gayly, the heavy wagons started off at a full gallop, and the beggars said, "May your graces go with God!"

It was the end of July, and the sky was blue and cloudless. The fine, soft light of the afternoon was falling on the tawny slopes and the close-reaped fields. The harvest was over. In the fields on either side they were threshing their grain, not as in the outside world, with the whirring of loud and swift machinery, nor even with the active and lively swinging of flails; but in the open air, under the warm sky, the cattle were lazily treading out the corn on the bare ground, to be winnowed by the wandering wind. No change from the time of Solomon. Through an infinity of ages, ever since corn and cattle were, the Iberian farmer in this very spot had driven his beasts over his crop, and never dreamed of a better way of doing the work.

Not only does the Spaniard not seek for improvements, he utterly despises and rejects them. The poorer classes especially, who would find an enormous advantage in increased production, lightening their hard lot by a greater plenty of the means of life, regard every introduction of improved machinery as a blow at the rights of labor. When many years ago a Dutch vintner went to Valdepenas and so greatly improved the manufacture of that excellent but ill-made wine that its price immediately rose in the Madrid market, he was mobbed and plundered by his ignorant neighbors, because, as they said, he was laboring to make wine dearer. In every attempt which has been made to manufacture improved machinery in Spain, the greatest care has to be taken to prevent the workmen from maliciously damaging the works, which they imagine are to take the bread from the mouths of their children.

So strong is this feeling in every department of national life, that the mayoral who drove our spanking nine-in-hand received with very ill humor our suggestion that the time could be greatly shortened by a Fell railroad over the hills to La Granja. "What would become of nosotros?" he asked. And it really would seem a pity to annihilate so much picturesqueness and color at the bidding of mere utility. A gayly embroidered Andalusian jacket, bright scarlet silk waistcoat,—a rich wide belt, into which his long knife, the navaja, was jauntily thrust,—buckskin breeches, with Valentian stockings, which, as they are open at the bottom, have been aptly likened to a Spaniard's purse,—and shoes made of Murcian matting, composed his natty outfit. By his side on the box sat the zagal, his assistant, whose especial function seemed to be to swear at the cattle. I have heard some eloquent imprecation in my day. "Our army swore terribly" at Hilton Head. The objuration of the boatmen of the Mississippi is very vigorous and racy. But I have never assisted at a session of profanity so loud, so energetic, so original as that with which this Castilian postilion regaled us. The wonderful consistency and perseverance with which the role was sustained was worthy of a much better cause.

He began by yelling in a coarse, strident voice, "Arre! arre!" (Get up!) with a vicious emphasis on the final syllable. This is one of the Moorish words that have remained fixed like fossils in the language of the conquerors. Its constant use in the mouths of muleteers has given them the name of arrieros. This general admonition being addressed to the team at large, the zagal descended to details, and proceeded to vilipend the galloping beasts separately, beginning with the leader. He informed him, still in this wild, jerking scream, that he was a dog, that his mother's character was far from that of Caesar's wife, and that if more speed was not exhibited on this down grade, he would be forced to resort to extreme measures. At the mention of a whip, the tall male mule who led the team dashed gallantly off, and the diligence was soon enveloped in a cloud of dust. This seemed to excite our gay charioteer to the highest degree. He screamed lustily at his mules, addressing each personally by its name. "Andaluza, arre! Thou of Arragon, go! Beware the scourge, Manchega!" and every animal acknowledged the special attention by shaking its ears and bells and whisking its shaven tail, as the diligence rolled furiously over the dull drab plain.

For three hours the iron lungs of the muleteer knew no rest or pause. Several times in the journey we stopped at a post-station to change our cattle, but the same brazen throat sufficed for all the threatening and encouragement that kept them at the top of their speed. Before we arrived at our journey's end, however, he was hoarse as a raven, and kept one hand pressed to his jaw to reinforce the exhausted muscles of speech.

When the wide and dusty plain was passed, we began by a slow and winding ascent the passage of the Guadarrama. The road is an excellent one, and although so seldom used,—a few months only in the year,—it is kept in the most perfect repair. It is exclusively a summer road, being in the winter impassable with snow. It affords at every turn the most charming compositions of mountain and wooded valley. At intervals we passed a mounted guardia civil, who sat as motionless in his saddle as an equestrian statue, and saluted as the coaches rattled by. And once or twice in a quiet nook by the roadside we came upon the lonely cross that marked the spot where a man had been murdered.

It was nearly sunset when we arrived at the summit of the pass. We halted to ask for a glass of water at the hut of a gray-haired woman on the mountain-top. It was given and received as always in this pious country, in the name of God. As we descended, the mules seemed to have gained new vigor from the prospect of an easy stretch of *facilis descensus,* and the zagal employed what was left of his voice in provoking them to speed by insulting remarks upon their lineage. The quick twilight fell as we entered a vast forest of pines that clothed the mountain-side. The enormous trees looked in the dim evening light like the forms of the Anakim, maimed with lightning but still defying heaven. Years of battle with the mountain winds had twisted them into every conceivable shape of writhing and distorted deformity. I never saw trees that so nearly conveyed the idea of being the visible prison of tortured dryads. Their trunks, white and glistening with oozing resin, added to the ghostly impression they created in the uncertain and failing light.

We reached the valley and rattled by a sleepy village, where we were greeted by a chorus of outraged curs whose beauty-sleep we had disturbed, and then began the slow ascent of the hill where St. Ildefonso stands. We had not gone far when we heard a pattering of hoofs and a ringing of sabres coming down the road to meet us. The diligence stopped, and the Introducer of Ambassadors jumped to the ground and announced, "El Regente del Reino!" It was the regent, the courteous and amiable Marshal Serrano, who had ridden out from the palace to welcome his guests, and who, after hasty salutations, galloped back to La Granja, where we soon arrived.

We were assigned the apartments usually given to the papal nuncio, and slept with an episcopal peace of mind. In the morning, as we were walking about the gardens, we saw looking from the palace window one of the most accomplished gentlemen and diplomatists of the new regime. He descended and did the honors of the place. The system of gardens and fountains is enormous. It is evidently modelled upon Versailles, but the copy is in many respects finer than the original. The peculiarity of the site, while offering great difficulties, at the same time enhances the triumph of success. This is a garden taught to bloom upon a barren mountain-side. The earth in which these trees are planted was brought from those dim plains in the distance on the backs of men and mules. The pipes that supply these innumerable fountains were laid on the bare rocks and the soil was thrown over them. Every tree was guarded and watched like a baby. There was probably never a garden that grew under such circumstances,—but the result is superb. The fountains are fed by a vast reservoir in the mountain, and the water they throw into the bright air is as clear as morning dew. Every alley and avenue is a vista that ends in a vast picture of shaggy hills or far-off plains,—while behind the royal gardens towers the lordly peak of the Penalara, thrust eight thousand feet into the thin blue ether.

The palace has its share of history. It witnessed the abdication of the uxorious bigot Philip V. in 1724, and his resumption of the crown the next year at the instance of his proud and turbulent Parmesan wife. His bones rest in the church here, as he hated the Austrian line too intensely to share with them the gorgeous crypt of the Escorial. His wife, Elizabeth Farnese, lies under the same gravestone with him, as if unwilling to forego even in death that tremendous influence which her vigorous vitality had always exercised over his wavering and sensual nature. "Das Ewig-Weibliche" masters and guides him still.

This retreat in the autumn of 1832 was the scene of a prodigious exhibition of courage and energy on the part of another Italian woman, Dona Louisa Carlota de Borbon. Ferdinand VIL, his mind weakened by illness, and influenced by his ministers, had proclaimed his brother Don Carlos heir to the throne, to the exclusion of his own infant daughter. His wife, Queen Christine, broken down by the long conflict, had given way in despair. But her sister, Dona Louisa Carlota, heard of the news in the south of Spain, and, leaving her babies at *Cadiz* (two little urchins, one of whom was to be king consort, and the other was to fall by his cousin Montpensier's hand in the field of Carabanchel), she posted without a moment's pause for rest or sleep over mountains and plains from the sea to La Granja. She fought with the lackeys and the ministers twenty-four hours before she could see her sister the queen. Having breathed into Christine her own invincible spirit, they succeeded, after endless pains, in reaching the king. Obstinate as the weak often are, he refused at first to listen to them; but by their womanly wiles, their Italian policy, their magnetic force, they at last brought him to revoke his decree in favor of Don Carlos and to recognize the right of his daughter to the crown. Then, terrible in her triumph, Dona Louisa Carlota sent for the Minister Calomarde, overwhelmed him with the coarsest and most furious abuse, and, unable to confine her victorious rage and hate to words alone, she slapped the astounded minister in the face. Calomarde, trembling with rage, bowed and said, "A white hand cannot offend."

There is nothing stronger than a woman's weakness, or weaker than a woman's strength.

A few years later, when Ferdinand was in his grave, and the baby Isabel reigned under the regency of Christine, a movement in favor of the constitution of 1812 burst out, where revolutions generally do, in the south, and spread rapidly over the contiguous provinces. The infection gained the troops of the royal guard at La Granja, and they surrounded the palace bawling for the constitution. The regentess, with a proud reliance upon her own power, ordered them to send a deputation to her apartment. A dozen of the mutineers came in, and demanded the constitution.

"What is that?" asked the queen.

They looked at each other and cudgelled their brains. They had never thought of that before.

"Caramba!" said they. "We don't know. They say it is a good thing, and will raise our pay and make salt cheaper."

Their political economy was somewhat flimsy, but they had the bayonets, and the queen was compelled to give way and proclaim the constitution.

I must add one trifling reminiscence more of La Granja, which has also its little moral. A friend of mine, a colonel of engineers, in the summer before the revolution, was standing before the palace with some officers, when a mean-looking cur ran past.

"What an ugly dog!" said the colonel.

"Hush!" replied another, with an awe-struck face. "That is the dog of his royal highness the Prince of Asturias."

The colonel unfortunately had a logical mind, and failed to see that ownership had any bearing on a purely aesthetic question. He defined his position. "I do not think the dog is ugly because he belongs to the prince. I only mean the prince has an ugly dog."

The window just above them slammed, and another officer came up and said that the Adversary was to pay. "THE QUEEN was at the window and heard every word you said."

An hour after the colonel received an order from the commandant of the
place, revoking his leave of absence and ordering him to duty in Madrid.
It is not very surprising that this officer was at the Bridge of Alcolea.

At noon the day grew dark with clouds, and the black storm-wreath came down over the mountains. A terrific fire of artillery resounded for a half-hour in the craggy peaks about us, and a driving shower passed over palace and gardens. Then the sun came out again, the pleasure-grounds were fresher and greener than ever, and the visitors thronged in the court of the palace to see the fountains in play. The regent led the way on foot. The general followed in a pony phaeton, and ministers, adjutants, and the population of the district trooped along in a party-colored mass.

It was a good afternoon's work to visit all the fountains. They are twenty-six in number, strewn over the undulating grounds. People who visit Paris usually consider a day of Grandes Eaux at Versailles the last word of this species of costly trifling. But the waters at Versailles bear no comparison with those of La Granja. The sense is fatigued and bewildered here with their magnificence and infinite variety. The vast reservoir in the bosom of the mountain, filled with the purest water, gives a possibility of more superb effects than have been attained anywhere else in the world. The Fountain of the Winds is one, where a vast mass of water springs into the air from the foot of a great cavernous rock; there is a succession of exquisite cascades called the Race-Course, filled with graceful statuary; a colossal group of Apollo slaying the Python, who in his death agony bleeds a torrent of water; the Basket of Flowers, which throws up a system of forty jets; the great single jet called Fame, which leaps one hundred and thirty feet into the air, a Niagara reversed; and the crowning glory of the garden, the Baths of Diana, an immense stage scene in marble and bronze, crowded with nymphs and hunting-parties, wild beasts and birds, and everywhere the wildest luxuriance of spouting waters. We were told that it was one of the royal caprices of a recent tenant of the palace to emulate her chaste proto-type of the silver bow by choosing this artistic basin for her ablutions, a sufficient number of civil guards being posted to prevent the approach of Castilian Actaeons. Ford aptly remarks of these extravagant follies: "The yoke of building kings is grievous, and especially when, as St. Simon said of Louis XIV. and his Versailles, 'Il se plut a tyranniser la nature.'"

As the bilious Philip paused before this mass of sculptured extravagance, he looked at it a moment with evident pleasure. Then he thought of the bill, and whined, "Thou hast amused me three minutes and hast cost me three millions."

To do Philip justice, he did not allow the bills to trouble him much. He died owing forty-five million piastres, which his dutiful son refused to pay. When you deal with Bourbons, it is well to remember the Spanish proverb, "A sparrow in the hand is better than a bustard on the wing."

We wasted an hour in walking through the palace. It is, like all palaces, too fine and dreary to describe. Miles of drawing-rooms and boudoirs, with an infinity of tapestry and gilt chairs, all the apartments haunted by the demon of ennui. All idea of comfort is sacrificed to costly glitter and flimsy magnificence. Some fine paintings were pining in exile on the desolate walls. They looked homesick for the Museum, where they could be seen of men.

The next morning we drove down the mountain and over the rolling plain to the fine old city of Segovia. In point of antiquity and historic interest it is inferior to no town in Spain. It has lost its ancient importance as a seat of government and a mart of commerce.

Its population is now not more than eleven thousand. Its manufactures have gone to decay. Its woollen works, which once employed fourteen thousand persons and produced annually twenty-five thousand pieces of cloth, now sustain a sickly existence and turn out not more than two hundred pieces yearly. Its mint, which once spread over Spain a Danaean shower of ounces and dollars, is now reduced to the humble office of striking copper cuartos. More than two centuries ago this decline began. Boisel, who was there in 1669, speaks of the city as "presque desert et fort pauvre." He mentions as a mark of the general unthrift that the day he arrived there was no bread in town until two o'clock in the afternoon, "and no one was astonished at it."

Yet even in its poverty and rags it has the air of a town that has seen better days. Tradition says it was founded by Hercules. It was an important city of the Roman Empire, and a great capital in the days of the Arab monarchy. It was the court of the star-gazing King Alonso the Wise. Through a dozen centuries it was the flower of the mountains of Castile. Each succeeding age and race beautified and embellished it, and each, departing, left the trace of its passage in the abiding granite of its monuments. The Romans left the glorious aqueduct, that work of demigods who scorned to mention it in their histories; its mediaeval bishops bequeathed to later times their ideas of ecclesiastical architecture; and the Arabs the science of fortification and the industrial arts.

Its very ruin and decay makes it only more precious to the traveller. There are here none of the modern and commonplace evidences of life and activity that shock the artistic sense in other towns. All is old, moribund, and picturesque. It lies here in the heart of the Guadarramas, lost and forgotten by the civilization of the age, muttering in its senile dream of the glories of an older world. It has not vitality enough to attract a railroad, and so is only reached by a long and tiresome journey by diligence. Its solitude is rarely intruded upon by the impertinent curious, and the red back of Murray is a rare apparition in its winding streets.

Yet those who come are richly repaid. One does not quickly forget the impression produced by the first view of the vast aqueduct, as you drive into the town from La Granja. It comes upon you in an instant,—the two great ranges of superimposed arches, over one hundred feet high, spanning the ravine-like suburb from the outer hills to the Alcazar. You raise your eyes from the market-place, with its dickering crowd, from the old and squalid houses clustered like shot rubbish at the foot of the chasm, to this grand and soaring wonder of utilitarian architecture, with something of a fancy that it was never made, that it has stood there since the morning of the world. It has the lightness and the strength, the absence of ornament and the essential beauty, the vastness and the perfection, of a work of nature.

It is one of those gigantic works of Trajan, so common in that magnificent age that Roman authors do not allude to it. It was built to bring the cool mountain water of the Sierra Fonfria a distance of nine miles through the hills, the gulches, and the pine forests of Valsain, and over the open plain to the thirsty city of Segovia. The aqueduct proper runs from the old tower of Caseron three thousand feet to the reservoir where the water deposits its sand and sediment, and thence begins the series of one hundred and nineteen arches, which traverse three thousand feet more and pass the valley, the arrabal, and reach the citadel. It is composed of great blocks of granite, so perfectly framed and fitted that not a particle of mortar or cement is employed in the construction.

The wonder of the work is not so much in its vastness or its beauty as in its tremendous solidity and duration. A portion of it had been cut away by barbarous armies during the fifteenth century, and in the reign of Isabella the Catholic the monk-architect of the Parral, Juan Escovedo, the greatest builder of his day in Spain, repaired it. These repairs have themselves twice needed repairing since then. Marshal Ney, when he came to this portion of the monument, exclaimed, "Here begins the work of men's hands."

The true Segovian would hoot at you if you assigned any mortal paternity to the aqueduct. He calls it the Devil's Bridge, and tells you this story. The Evil One was in love with a pretty girl of the upper town, and full of protestations of devotion. The fair Segovian listened to him one evening, when her plump arms ached with the work of bringing water from the ravine, and promised eyes of favor if his Infernal Majesty would build an aqueduct to her door before morning. He worked all night, like the Devil, and the maiden, opening her black eyes at sunrise, saw him putting the last stone in the last arch, as the first ray of the sun lighted on his shining tail. The Church, we think very unfairly, decided that he had failed, and released the coquettish contractor from her promise; and it is said the Devil has never trusted a Sego-vian out of his sight again.

The bartizaned keep of the Moorish Alcazar is perched on the western promontory of the city that guards the meeting of the streams Eresma and Clamores. It has been in the changes of the warring times a palace, a fortress, a prison (where our friend—everybody's friend—Gil Blas was once confined), and of late years a college of artillery. In one of its rooms Alonso the Wise studied the heavens more than was good for his orthodoxy, and from one of its windows a lady of the court once dropped a royal baby, of the bad blood of Trasta-mara. Henry of Trastamara will seem more real if we connect him with fiction. He was the son of "La Favorita," who will outlast all legitimate princesses, in the deathless music of Donizetti.

Driving through a throng of beggars that encumbered the carriage wheels as grasshoppers sometimes do the locomotives on a Western railway, we came to the fine Gothic Cathedral, built by Gil de Ontanon, father and son, in the early part of the sixteenth century. It is a delight to the eyes; the rich harmonious color of the stone, the symmetry of proportion, the profuse opulence and grave finish of the details. It was built in that happy era of architecture when a builder of taste and culture had all the past of Gothic art at his disposition, and before the degrading influence of the Jesuits appeared in the churches of Europe. Within the Cathedral is remarkably airy and graceful in effect. A most judicious use has been made of the exquisite salmon-colored marbles of the country in the great altar and the pavement.

We were met by civil ecclesiastics of the foundation and shown the beauties and the wonders of the place. Among much that is worthless, there is one very impressive Descent from the Cross by Juan de Juni, of which that excellent Mr. Madoz says "it is worthy to rank with the best masterpieces of Raphael or—Mengs;" as if one should say of a poet that he was equal to Shakespeare or Southey.

We walked through the cloisters and looked at the tombs. A flood of warm light poured through the graceful arches and lit up the trees in the garden and set the birds to singing, and made these cloisters pleasanter to remember than they usually are. Our attendant priest told us, with an earnest credulity that was very touching, the story of Maria del Salto, Mary of the Leap, whose history was staring at us from the wall. She was a Jewish lady, whose husband had doubts of her discretion, and so threw her from a local Tarpeian rock. As she fell she invoked the Virgin, and came down easily, sustained, as you see in the picture, by her faith and her petticoats.

As we parted from the good fathers and entered our carriages at the door of the church, the swarm of mendicants had become an army. The word had doubtless gone through the city of the outlandish men who had gone into the Cathedral with whole coats, and the result was a *levee en masse* of the needy. Every coin that was thrown to them but increased the clamor, as it confirmed them in their idea of the boundless wealth and munificence of the givers. We recalled the profound thought of Emerson, "If the rich were only as rich as the poor think them!"

At last we drove desperately away through the ragged and screaming throng. We passed by the former home of the Jeronomite monks of the Parral, which was once called an earthly paradise, and in later years has been a pen for swine; past crumbling convents and ruined churches; past the charming Romanesque San Millan, girdled with its round-arched cloisters; the granite palace of his Reverence the Bishop of Segovia, and the elegant tower of St. Esteban, where the Roman is dying and the Gothic is dawning; and every step of the route is a study and a joy to the antiquarian.

But though enriched by all these legacies of an immemorial past, there seems no hope, no future for Segovia. It is as dead as the cities of the Plain. Its spindles have rusted into silence. Its gay company is gone. Its streets are too large for the population, and yet they swarm with beggars. I had often heard it compared in outline to a ship,— the sunrise astern and the prow pointing westward,—and as we drove away that day and I looked back to the receding town, it seemed to me like a grand hulk of some richly laden galleon, aground on the rock that holds it, alone, abandoned to its fate among the barren billows of the tumbling ridges, its crew tired out with struggling and apathetic in despair, mocked by the finest air and the clearest sunshine that ever shone, and gazing always forward to the new world and the new times hidden in the rosy sunset, which they shall never see.

THE CITY OF THE VISIGOTHS

Emilio Castelar said to me one day, "Toledo is the most remarkable city in Spain. You will find there three strata of glories,—Gothic, Arab, and Castilian,—and an upper crust of beggars and silence."

I went there in the pleasantest time of the year, the first days of June. The early harvest was in progress, and the sunny road ran through golden fields which were enlivened by the reapers gathering in their grain with shining sickles. The borders of the Tagus were so cool and fresh that it was hard to believe one was in the arid land of Castile. From Madrid to Aranjuez you meet the usual landscapes of dun hillocks and pale-blue vegetation, such as are only seen in nature in Central Spain, and only seen in art on the matchless canvas of Velazquez. But from the time you cross the tawny flood of the Tagus just north of Aranjuez, the valley is gladdened by its waters all the way to the Primate City.

I am glad I am not writing a guide-book, and do not feel any responsibility resting upon me of advising the gentle reader to stop at Aranjuez or to go by on the other side. There is a most amiable and praiseworthy class of travellers who feel a certain moral necessity impelling them to visit every royal abode within their reach. They always see precisely the same things,—some thousand of gilt chairs, some faded tapestry and marvellous satin upholstery, a room in porcelain, and a room in imitation of some other room somewhere else, and a picture or two by that worthy and tedious young man, Raphael Mengs. I knew I would see all these things at Aranjuez, and so contented myself with admiring its pretty site, its stone-cornered brick facade, its high-shouldered French roof, and its general air of the Place Royale, from the outside. The gardens are very pleasant, and lonely enough for the most philosophic stroller. A clever Spanish writer says of them, "They are sombre as the thoughts of Philip II., mysterious and gallant as the pleasures of Philip IV." To a revolutionary mind, it is a certain pleasure to remember that this was the scene of the *emeute* that drove Charles IV. from his throne, and the Prince of Peace from his queen's boudoir. Ferdinand VII., the turbulent and restless Prince of Asturias, reaped the immediate profit of his father's abdication; but the two worthless creatures soon called in Napoleon to decide the squabble, which he did in his leonine way by taking the crown away from both of them and handing it over for safe-keeping to his lieutenant brother Joseph. Honor among thieves! — a silly proverb, as one readily sees if he falls into their hands, or reads the history of kings.

If Toledo had been built, by some caprice of enlightened power, especially for a show city, it could not be finer in effect. In detail, it is one vast museum. In ensemble, it stands majestic on its hills, with its long lines of palaces and convents terraced around the rocky slope, and on the height the soaring steeples of a swarm of churches piercing the blue, and the huge cube of the Alcazar crowning the topmost crest, and domineering the scene. The magnificent zigzag road which leads up the steep hillside from the bridge of Alcantara gives an indefinable impression, as of the lordly ramp of some fortress of impossible extent.

This road is new, and in perfect condition. But do not imagine you can judge the city by the approaches. When your carriage has mounted the hill and passed the evening promenade of the Toledans, the quaint triangular Place, — I had nearly called it Square, — "waking laughter in indolent reviewers," the Zocodover, you are lost in the dae-dalian windings of the true streets of Toledo, where you can touch the walls on either side, and where two carriages could no more pass each other than two locomotives could salute and go by on the same track. This interesting experiment, which is so common in our favored land, could never be tried in Toledo, as I believe there is only one turnout in the city, a minute omnibus with striped linen hangings at the sides, driven by a young Castilian whose love of money is the root of much discussion when you pay his bill. It is a most remarkable establishment. The horses can cheerfully do their mile in fifteen or twenty minutes, but they make more row about it than a high-pressure Mississippi steamer; and the crazy little trap is noisier in proportion to its size than anything I have ever seen, except perhaps an Indiana tree-toad. If you make an excursion outside the walls, the omnibus, noise and all, is inevitable;

let it come. But inside the city you must walk; the slower the better, for every door is a study.

It is hard to conceive that this was once a great capital with a population of two hundred thousand souls. You can easily walk from one end of the city to the other in less than half an hour, and the houses that remain seem comfortably filled by eighteen thousand inhabitants. But in this narrow space once swarmed that enormous and busy multitude. The city was walled about by powerful stone ramparts, which yet stand in all their massy perfection. So there could have been no suburbs. This great aggregation of humanity lived and toiled on the crests and in the wrinkles of the seven hills we see to-day. How important were the industries of the earlier days we can guess from the single fact that John of Padilla, when he rose in defence of municipal liberty in the time of Charles V., drew in one day from the teeming workshops twenty thousand fighting men. He met the usual fate of all Spanish patriots, shameful and cruel death. His palace was razed to the ground. Successive governments, in shifting fever-fits of liberalism and absolutism, have set up and pulled down his statue. But his memory is loved and honored, and the example of this noblest of the comuneros impresses powerfully to-day the ardent young minds of the new Spain.

Your first walk is of course to the Cathedral, the Primate Church of the kingdom. Besides its ecclesiastical importance, it is well worthy of notice in itself. It is one of the purest specimens of Gothic architecture in existence, and is kept in an admirable state of preservation. Its situation is not the most favorable. It is approached by a network of descending streets, all narrow and winding, as streets were always built under the intelligent rule of the Moors. They preferred to be cool in summer and sheltered in winter, rather than to lay out great deserts of boulevards, the haunts of sunstroke and pneumonia. The site of the Cathedral was chosen from strategic reasons by St. Eugene, who built there his first Episcopal Church. The Moors made a mosque of it when they conquered Castile, and the fastidious piety of St. Ferdinand would not permit him to worship in a shrine thus profaned. He tore down the old church and laid, in 1227, the foundations of this magnificent structure, which was two centuries after his death in building. There is, however, great unity of purpose and execution in this Cathedral, due doubtless to the fact that the architect Perez gave fifty years of his long life to the superintendence of the early work. Inside and outside it is marked by a grave and harmonious majesty. The great western facade is enriched with three splendid portals,—the side ones called the doors of Hell and Judgment; and the central a beautiful ogival arch divided into two smaller ones, and adorned with a lavish profusion of delicately sculptured figures of saints and prophets; on the chaste and severe cornice above, a group of spirited busts represents the Last Supper. There are five other doors to the temple, of which the door of the Lions is the finest, and just beside it a heavy Ionic portico in the most detestable taste indicates the feeling and culture that survived in the reign of Charles IV.

To the north of the west facade rises the massive tower. It is not among the tallest in the world, being three hundred and twenty-four feet high, but is very symmetrical and impressive. In the preservation of its pyramidal purpose it is scarcely inferior to that most consummate work, the tower of St. Stephen's in Vienna. It is composed of three superimposed structures, gradually diminishing in solidity and massiveness from the square base to the high-springing octagonal spire, garlanded with thorny crowns. It is balanced at the south end of the facade by the pretty cupola and lantern of the Mozarabic Chapel, the work of the Greek Theotocopouli.

But we soon grow tired of the hot glare of June, and pass in a moment into the cool twilight vastness of the interior, refreshing to body and soul. Five fine naves, with eighty-four pillars formed each of sixteen graceful columns,—the entire edifice measuring four hundred feet in length and two hundred feet in breadth,—a grand and shadowy temple grove of marble and granite. At all times the light is of an unearthly softness and purity, toned by the exquisite windows and rosaces. But as evening draws on, you should linger till the sacristan grows peremptory, to watch the gorgeous glow of the western sunlight on the blazing roses of the portals, and the marvellous play of rich shadows and faint gray lights in the eastern chapels, where the grand aisles sweep in their perfect curves around the high altar. A singular effect is here created by the gilded organ pipes thrust out horizontally from the choir. When the powerful choral anthems of the church peal out over the kneeling multitude, it requires little fancy to imagine them the golden trumpets of concealed archangels, who would be quite at home in that incomparable choir.

If one should speak of all the noteworthy things you meet in this Cathedral, he would find himself in danger of following in the footsteps of Mr. Parro, who wrote a handbook of Toledo, in which seven hundred and forty-five pages are devoted to a hasty sketch of the basilica. For five hundred years enormous wealth and fanatical piety have worked together and in rivalry to beautify this spot. The boundless riches of the Church and the boundless superstition of the laity have left their traces here in every generation in forms of magnificence and beauty. Each of the chapels—and there are twenty-one of them—is a separate masterpiece in its way. The finest are those of Santiago and St. Ildefonso,—the former built by the famous Constable Alvaro de Luna as a burial-place for himself and family, and where he and his wife lie in storied marble; and the other commemorating that celebrated visit of the Virgin to the bishop, which is the favorite theme of the artists and ecclesiastical gossips of Spain.

There was probably never a morning call which gave rise to so much talk. It was not the first time the Virgin had come to Toledo. This was always a favorite excursion of hers. She had come from time to time, escorted by St. Peter, St. Paul, and St. James. But on the morning in question, which was not long after Bishop Ildefonso had written his clever treatise, "De Virginitate Stae Mariae," the Queen of Heaven came down to matin prayers, and, taking the bishop's seat, listened to the sermon with great edification. After service she presented him with a nice new chasuble, as his own was getting rather shabby, made of "cloth of heaven," in token of her appreciation of his spirited pamphlet in her defence. This chasuble still exists in a chest in Asturias. If you open the chest, you will not see it; but this only proves the truth of the miracle, for the chroniclers say the sacred vestment is invisible to mortal eyes.

But we have another and more palpable proof of the truth of the history. The slab of marble on which the feet of the celestial visitor alighted is still preserved in the Cathedral in a tidy chapel built on the very spot where the avatar took place. The slab is enclosed in red jasper and guarded by an iron grating, and above it these words of the Psalmist are engraved in the stone, *Adorabimus in loco ubi steterunt pedes ejus.*

This story is cut in marble and carved in wood and drawn upon brass and painted upon canvas, in a thousand shapes and forms all over Spain. You see in the Museum at Madrid a picture by Murillo devoted to this idle fancy of a cunning or dreaming priest. The subject was unworthy of the painter, and the result is what might have been expected, — a picture of trivial and mundane beauty, without the least suggestion of spirituality.

But there can be no doubt of the serious, solemn earnestness with which the worthy Castilians from that day to this believe the romance. They came up in groups and families, touching their fingers to the sacred slab and kissing them reverentially with muttered prayers. A father would take the first kiss himself, and pass his consecrated finger around among his awe-struck babes, who were too brief to reach to the grating. Even the aged verger who showed us the shrine, who was so frail and so old that we thought he might be a ghost escaped from some of the mediaeval tombs in the neighborhood, never passed that pretty white-and-gold chapel without sticking in his thumb and pulling out a blessing.

A few feet from this worship-worn stone, a circle drawn on one of the marble flags marks the spot where Santa Leocadia also appeared to this same favored Ildefonso and made her compliments on his pamphlet. Was ever author so happy in his subject and his gentle readers? The good bishop evidently thought the story of this second apparition might be considered rather a heavy draught on the credulity of his flock, so he whipped out a convenient knife and cut off a piece of her saint-ship's veil, which clinched the narrative and struck doubters dumb. That great king and crazy relic-hunter, Philip II., saw this rag in his time with profound emotion, — this tiger heart, who could order the murder of a thousand innocent beings without a pang.

There is another chapel in this Cathedral which preaches forever its silent condemnation of Spanish bigotry to deaf ears. This is the Mozarabic Chapel, sacred to the celebration of the early Christian rite of Spain. During the three centuries of Moorish domination the enlightened and magnanimous conquerors guaranteed to those

Christians who remained within their lines the free exercise of all their rights, including perfect freedom of worship. So that side by side the mosque and the church worshipped God each in its own way without fear or wrong. But when Alonso VI. recaptured the city in the eleventh century, he wished to establish uniformity of worship, and forbade the use of the ancient liturgy in Toledo. That which the heathen had respected the Catholic outraged. The great Cardinal Ximenez restored the primitive rite and devoted this charming chapel to its service. How ill a return was made for Moorish tolerance we see in the infernal treatment they afterwards received from king and Church. They made them choose between conversion and death. They embraced Christianity to save their lives. Then the priests said, "Perhaps this conversion is not genuine! Let us send the heathen away out of our sight." One million of the best citizens of Spain were thus torn from their homes and landed starving on the wild African coast. And Te Deums were sung in the churches for this triumph of Catholic unity. From that hour Spain has never prospered. It seems as if she were lying ever since under the curse of these breaking hearts.

Passing by a world of artistic beauties which never tire the eyes, but soon would tire the chronicler and reader, stepping over the broad bronze slab in the floor which covers the dust of the haughty primate Porto Carrero, but which bears neither name nor date, only this inscription of arrogant humility, HIC JACET PULVIS CINIS ET NIHIL, we walk into the verdurous and cheerful Gothic cloisters. They occupy the site of the ancient Jewish markets, and the zealous prelate Tenorio, cousin to the great lady's man Don Juan, could think of no better way of acquiring the ground than that of stirring up the mob to burn the houses of the heretics. A fresco that adorns the gate explains the means employed, adding insult to the old injury. It is a picture of a beautiful child hanging upon a cross; a fiendish-looking Jew, on a ladder beside him, holds in his hand the child's heart, which he has just taken from his bleeding breast; he holds the dripping knife in his teeth. This brutal myth was used for centuries with great effect by the priesthood upon the mob whenever they wanted a Jew's money or his blood. Even to-day the old poison has not lost its power. This very morning I heard under my window loud and shrill voices. I looked out and saw a group of brown and ragged women, with babies in their arms, discussing the news from Madrid. The Protestants, they said, had begun to steal Catholic children. They talked themselves into a fury. Their elf-locks hung about their fierce black eyes. The sinews of their lean necks worked tensely in their voluble rage. Had they seen our mild missionary at that moment, whom all men respect and all children instinctively love, they would have torn him in pieces in their Maenad fury, and would have thought they were doing their duty as mothers and Catholics.

This absurd and devilish charge was seriously made in a Madrid journal, the organ of the Moderates, and caused great fermentation for several days, street rows, and debates in the Cortes, before the excitement died away. Last summer, in the old Murcian town of Lorca, an English gentleman, who had been several weeks in the place, was attacked and nearly killed by a mob, who insisted that he was engaged in the business of stealing children, and using their spinal marrow for lubricating telegraph wires! What a picture of blind and savage ignorance is here presented! It reminds us of that sad and pitiful "blood-bath revolt" of Paris, where the wretched mob rose against the wretched tyrant Louis XV., accusing him of bathing in the blood of children to restore his own wasted and corrupted energies.

Toledo is a city where you should eschew guides and trust implicitly to chance in your wanderings. You can never be lost; the town is so small that a short walk always brings you to the river or the wall, and there you can take a new departure. If you do not know where you are going, you have every moment the delight of some unforeseen pleasure. There is not a street in Toledo that is not rich in treasures of architecture,—hovels that once were marvels of building, balconies of curiously wrought iron, great doors with sculptured posts and lintels, with gracefully finished hinges, and studded with huge nails whose fanciful heads are as large as billiard balls. Some of these are still handsome residences, but most have fallen into neglect and abandonment. You may find a beggar installed in the ruined palace of a Moorish prince, a cobbler at work in the pleasure-house of a Castilian conqueror. The graceful carvings are mutilated and destroyed, the delicate arabesques are smothered and hidden under a triple coat of whitewash. The most beautiful Moorish house in the city, the so-called Taller del Moro, where the grim governor of Huesca invited four hundred influential gentlemen of the province to a political dinner, and cut off all their heads as they entered (if we may believe the chronicle, which we do not), is now empty and rapidly going to ruin. The exquisite panelling of the walls, the endlessly varied stucco work that seems to have been wrought by the deft fingers of ingenious fairies, is shockingly broken and marred. Gigantic cacti look into the windows from the outer court. A gay pomegranate-tree flings its scarlet blossoms in on the ruined floor. Rude little birds have built their nests in the beautiful fretted rafters, and flutter in and out as busy as brokers. But of all the feasting and loving and plotting these lovely walls beheld in that strange age that seems like fable now,—the vivid, intelligent, scientific, tolerant age of the Moors,—even the memory has perished utterly and forever.

We strolled away aimlessly from this beautiful desolation, and soon came out upon the bright and airy Paseo del Transito. The afternoon sunshine lay warm on the dull brown suburb, but a breeze blew freshly through the dark river-gorge, and we sat upon the stone benches bordering the bluff and gave ourselves up to the scene. To the right were the ruins of the Roman bridge and the Moorish mills; to the left the airy arch of San Martin's bridge spanned the bounding torrent, and far beyond stretched the vast expanse of the green valley refreshed by the river, and rolling in rank waves of verdure to the blue hills of Guadalupe. Below us on the slippery rocks that lay at the foot of the sheer cliffs, some luxurious fishermen reclined, idly watching their idle lines. The hills stretched away, ragged and rocky, dotted with solitary towers and villas.

A squad of beggars rapidly gathered, attracted by the gracious faces of Las Senoras. Begging seems almost the only regular industry of Toledo. Besides the serious professionals, who are real artists in studied misery and ingenious deformity, all the children in town occasionally leave their marbles and their leap-frog to turn an honest penny by amateur mendicancy.

A chorus of piteous whines went up. But La Senora was firm. She checked the ready hands of the juveniles. "Children should not be encouraged to pursue this wretched life. We should give only to blind men, because here is a great and evident affliction; and to old women, because they look so lonely about the boots." The exposition was so subtle and logical that it admitted no reply. The old women and the blind men shuffled away with their pennies, and we began to chaff the sturdy and rosy children.

A Spanish beggar can bear anything but banter. He is a keen physiognomist, and selects his victims with unerring acumen. If you storm or scowl at him, he knows he is making you uncomfortable, and hangs on like a burr. But if you laugh at him, with good humor, he is disarmed. A friend of mine reduced to confusion one of the most unabashed mendicants in Castile by replying to his whining petition, politely and with a beaming smile, "No, thank you. I never eat them." The beggar is far from considering his employment a degrading one. It is recognized by the Church, and the obligation of this form of charity especially inculcated. The average Spaniard regards it as a sort of tax to be as readily satisfied as a toll-fee. He will often stop and give a beggar a cent, and wait for the change in maravedises. One day, at the railway station, a muscular rogue approached me and begged for alms. I offered him my *sac-de-nuit* to carry a block or two. He drew himself up proudly and said, "I beg your pardon, sir; I am no Gallician." An old woman came up with a basket on her arm. "Can it be possible in this far country," said La Senora, "or are these—yes, they are, deliberate peanuts." With a penny we bought unlimited quantities of this levelling edible, and with them the devoted adherence of the aged merchant. She immediately took charge of our education. We must see Santa Maria la Blanca,—it was a beautiful thing; so was the Transito. Did we see those men and women grubbing in the hillside? They were digging bones to sell at the station. Where did the bones come from? Quien sabe? Those dust-heaps have been there since King Wamba. Come, we must go and see the Churches of Mary before it grew dark. And the zealous old creature marched away with us to the synagogue built by Samuel Ben Levi, treasurer to that crowned panther, Peter the Cruel. This able financier built this fine temple to the God of his fathers out of his own purse. He was murdered for his money by his ungrateful lord, and his synagogue stolen by the Church. It now belongs to the order of Cala-trava.

But the other and older synagogue, now called Santa Maria la Blanca, is much more interesting. It stands in the same quarter, the suburb formerly occupied by the industrious and thriving Hebrews of the Middle Ages until the stupid zeal of the Catholic kings drove them out of Spain. The synagogue was built in the ninth century under the enlightened domination of the Moors. At the slaughter of the Jews in 1405 it became a church. It has passed through varying fortunes since then, having been hospital, hermitage, stable, and warehouse; but it is now under the care of the provincial committee of art, and is somewhat decently restored. Its architecture is altogether Moorish. It has three aisles with thick octagonal columns supporting heavy horseshoe arches. The spandrels are curiously adorned with rich circular stucco figures. The soil you tread is sacred, for it was brought from Zion long before the Crusades; the cedar rafters above you preserve the memory and the odors of Lebanon.

A little farther west, on a fine hill overlooking the river, in the midst of the ruined palaces of the early kings, stands the beautiful votive church of San Juan de los Reyes. It was built by Ferdinand and Isabella, before the Columbus days, to commemorate a victory over their neighbors the Portuguese. During a prolonged absence of the king, the pious queen, wishing to prepare him a pleasant surprise, instead of embroidering a pair of impracticable slippers as a faithful young wife would do nowadays, finished this exquisite church by setting at work upon it some regiments of stone-cutters and builders. It is not difficult to imagine the beauty of the structure that greeted the king on his welcome home. For even now, after the storms of four centuries have beaten upon it, and the malignant hands of invading armies have used their utmost malice against it, it is still a won-drously perfect work of the Gothic inspiration.

We sat on the terrace benches to enjoy the light and graceful lines of the building, the delicately ornate door, the unique drapery of iron chains which the freed Christians hung here when delivered from the hands of the Moors. A lovely child, with pensive blue eyes fringed with long lashes, and the slow sweet smile of a Madonna, sat near us and sang to a soft, monotonous air a war-song of the Carlists. Her beauty soon attracted the artistic eyes of La Senora, and we learned she was named Francisca, and her baby brother, whose flaxen head lay heavily on her shoulder, was called Jesus Mary. She asked, Would we like to go into the church? She knew the sacristan and would go for him. She ran away like a fawn, the tow head of little Jesus tumbling dangerously about. She reappeared in a moment; she had disposed of mi nino, as she called it, and had found the sacristan. This personage was rather disappointing. A sacristan should be aged and mouldy, clothed in black of a decent shabbiness. This was a Toledan swell in a velvet shooting-jacket, and yellow peg-top trousers. However, he had the wit to confine himself to turning keys, and so we gradually recovered from the shock of the shooting-jacket.

The church forms one great nave, divided into four vaults enriched with wonderful stone lace-work. A superb frieze surrounds the entire nave, bearing in great Gothic letters an inscription narrating the foundation of the church. Everywhere the arms of Castile and Arragon, and the wedded ciphers of the Catholic kings. Statues of heralds start unexpectedly out from the face of the pillars. Fine as the church is, we cannot linger here long. The glory of San Juan is its cloisters. It may challenge the world to show anything so fine in the latest bloom and last development of Gothic art. One of the galleries is in ruins, — a sad witness of the brutality of armies. But the three others arc cnough to show how much of beauty was possible in that final age of pure Gothic building. The arches bear a double garland of leaves, of flowers, and of fruits, and among them are ramping and writhing and playing every figure of bird or beast or monster that man has seen or poet imagined. There are no two arches alike, and yet a most beautiful harmony pervades them all. In some the leaves are in profile, in others delicately spread upon the graceful columns and every vein displayed. I saw one window where a stone monkey sat reading his prayers, gowned and cowled, — an odd caprice of the tired sculptor. There is in this infinite variety of detail a delight that ends in something like fatigue. You cannot help feeling that this was naturally and logically the end of Gothic art. It had run its course. There was nothing left but this feverish quest of variety. It was in danger, after having gained such divine heights of invention, of degenerating into prettinesses and affectation.

But how marvellously fine it was at last! One must see it, as in these unequalled cloisters, half ruined, silent, and deserted, bearing with something of conscious dignity the blows of time and the ruder wrongs of men, to appreciate fully its proud superiority to all the accidents of changing taste and modified culture. It is only the truest art that can bear that test. The fanes of Paestum will always be more beautiful even than the magical shore on which they stand. The Parthenon, fixed like a battered coronet on the brow of the Acropolis, will always be the loveliest sight that Greece can offer to those who come sailing in from the blue Aegean. It is scarcely possible to imagine a condition of thought or feeling in which these master-works shall seem quaint or old-fashioned. They appeal, now and always, with that calm power of perfection, to the heart and eyes of every man born of woman.

The cloisters enclose a little garden just enough neglected to allow the lush dark ivy, the passionflowers, and the spreading oleanders to do their best in beautifying the place, as men have done their worst in marring it. The clambering vines seem trying to hide the scars of their hardly less perfect copies. Every arch is adorned with a soft and delicious drapery of leaves and tendrils; the fair and outraged child of art is cherished and caressed by the gracious and bountiful hands of Mother Nature.

As we came away, little Francisca plucked one of the five-pointed leaves of the passion-flowers and gave it to La Senora, saying reverentially, "This is the Hand of Our Blessed Lord!"

The sun was throned, red as a bacchanal king, upon the purple hills, as we descended the rocky declivity and crossed the bridge of St. Martin.

Our little Toledan maid came with us, talking and singing incessantly, like a sweet-voiced starling. We rested on the farther side and looked back at the towering city, glorious in the sunset, its spires aflame, its long lines of palace and convent clear in the level rays, its ruins softened in the gathering shadows, the lofty bridge hanging transfigured over the glowing river. Before us the crumbling walls and turrets of the Gothic kings ran down from the bluff to the water-side, its terrace overlooking the baths where, for his woe, Don Roderick saw Count Julian's daughter under the same inflammatory circumstances as those in which, from a Judaean housetop, Don David beheld Captain Uriah's wife. There is a great deal of human nature abroad in the world in all ages.

Little Francisca kept on chattering. "That is St. Martin's bridge. A girl jumped into the water last year. She was not a lady. She was in service. She was tired of living because she was in love. They found her three weeks afterwards; but, Santisima Maria! she was good for nothing then."

Our little maid was too young to have sympathy for kings or servant girls who die for love. She was a pretty picture as she sat there, her blue eyes and Madonna face turned to the rosy west, singing in her sweet child's voice her fierce little song of sedition and war: —

"Arriba los valientes!
Abajo tirania!
Pronto llegara el dia
  De la Restauracion.

Carlistas a caballo!
Soldados en Campana!
Viva el Rey de Espana,
  Don Carlos de Borbon!"

I cannot enumerate the churches of Toledo, — you find them in every street and by-way. In the palmy days of the absolute theocracy this narrow space contained more than a hundred churches and chapels. The province was gnawed by the cancer of sixteen monasteries of monks and twice as many convents of nuns, all crowded within these city walls. Fully one half the ground of the city was covered by religious buildings and mortmain property. In that age, when money meant ten times what it signifies now, the rent-roll of the Church in Toledo was forty millions of reals. There are even yet portions of the town where you find nothing but churches and convents. The grass grows green in the silent streets. You hear nothing but the chime of bells and the faint echoes of masses. You see on every side bolted doors and barred windows, and, gliding over the mossy pavements, the stealthy-stepping, long-robed priests.

I will only mention two more churches, and both of these converts from heathendom; both of them dedicated to San Cristo, for in the democracy of the calendar the Saviour is merely a saint, and reduced to the level of the rest. One is the old pretorian temple of the Romans, which was converted by King Sizebuto into a Christian church in the seventh century. It is a curious structure in brick and mortar, with an apsis and an odd arrangement of round arches sunken in the outer wall and still deeper pointed ones. It is famed as the resting-place of Saints Ildefonso and Leocadia, whom we have met before. The statue of the latter stands over the door graceful and pensive enough for a heathen muse. The little cloisters leading to the church are burial vaults. On one side lie the canonical dead and on the other the laity, with bright marble tablets and gilt inscriptions. In the court outside I noticed a flat stone marked *Ossuarium.* The sacristan told me this covered the pit where the nameless dead reposed, and when the genteel people in the gilt marble vaults neglected to pay their annual rent, they were taken out and tumbled in to moulder with the common clay.

This San Cristo de la Vega, St. Christ of the Plain, stands on the wide flat below the town, where you find the greater portion of the Roman remains. Heaps of crumbling composite stretched in an oval form over the meadow mark the site of the great circus. Green turf and fields of waving grain occupy the ground where once a Latin city stood. The Romans built on the plain. The Goths, following their instinct of isolation, fixed their dwelling on the steep and rugged rock. The rapid Tagus girdling the city like a horseshoe left only the declivity to the west to be defended, and the ruins of King Wamba's wall show with what jealous care that work was done. But the Moors, after they captured the city, apparently did little for its defence. A great suburb grew up in the course of ages outside the wall, and when the Christians recaptured Toledo in 1085, the first care of Alonso VI. was to build another wall, this time nearer the foot of the hill, taking inside all the accretion of these years. From that day to this that wall has held Toledo. The city has never reached, perhaps will never reach, the base of the steep rock on which it stands.

When King Alonso stormed the city, his first thought, in the busy half hour that follows victory, was to find some convenient place to say his prayers. Chance led him to a beautiful little Moorish mosque or oratory near the superb Puerta del Sol. He entered, gave thanks, and hung up his shield as a votive offering. This is the Church of San Cristo de la Luz. The shield of Alonso hangs there defying time for eight centuries, — a golden cross on a red field, — and the exquisite oratory, not much larger than a child's toy-house, is to-day one of the most charming specimens of Moorish art in Spain. Four square pillars support the roof, which is divided into five equal "half-orange" domes, each different from the others and each equally fascinating in its unexpected simplicity and grace. You cannot avoid a feeling of personal kindliness and respect for the refined and genial spirit who left this elegant legacy to an alien race and a hostile creed.

The Military College of Santa Cruz is one of the most precious specimens extant of those somewhat confused but beautiful results of the transition from florid Gothic to the Renaissance. The plateresque is young and modest, and seeks to please in this splendid monument by allying the innovating forms with the traditions of a school outgrown. There is an exquisite and touching reminiscence of the Gothic in the superb portal and the matchless group of the Invention of the Cross. All this fine facade is by that true and genuine artist, Enrique de Egas, the same who carved the grand Gate of the Lions, for which may the gate of paradise be open to him.

The inner court is surrounded by two stories of airy arcades, supported by slim Corinthian columns. In one corner is the most elaborate staircase in Spain. All the elegance and fancy of Arab and Renaissance art have been lavished upon this masterly work.

Santa Cruz was built for a hospital by that haughty Cardinal Mendoza, the Tertius Rex of Ferdinand and Isabella. It is now occupied by the military school, which receives six hundred cadets. They are under the charge of an inspector-general and a numerous staff of professors. They pay forty cents a day for their board. The instruction is gratuitous and comprehends a curriculum almost identical with that of West Point. It occupies, however, only three years.

The most considerable Renaissance structure in Toledo is the Royal Alcazar. It covers with its vast bulk the highest hilltop in the city. From the earliest antiquity this spot has been occupied by a royal palace or fortress. But the present structure was built by Charles V. and completed by Herrera for Philip II. Its north and south facades are very fine. The Alcazar seems to have been marked by fate. The Portuguese burned it in the last century, and Charles III. restored it just in time for the French to destroy it anew. Its indestructible walls alone remain. Now, after many years of ruinous neglect, the government has begun the work of restoration. The vast quadrangle is one mass of scaffolding and plaster dust. The grand staircase is almost finished again. In the course of a few years we may expect to see the Alcazar in a state worthy of its name and history. We would hope it might never again shelter a king. They have had their day there. Their line goes back so far into the mists of time that its beginning eludes our utmost search. The Roman drove out the unnamed chiefs of Iberia. The fair-haired Goth dispossessed the Italian. The Berber destroyed the Gothic monarchy. Castile and Leon fought their way down inch by inch through three centuries from Covadonga to Toledo, halfway in time and territory to Granada and the Midland Sea. And since then how many royal feet have trodden this breezy crest,—Sanchos and Henrys and Ferdinands,—the line broken now and then by a usurping uncle or a fratricide brother,—a red-handed bastard of Trastamara, a star-gazing Alonso, a plotting and praying Charles, and, after Philip, the dwindling scions of Austria and the nullities of Bourbon. This height has known as well the rustle of the trailing robes of queens,—Berenguela, Isabel the Catholic, and Juana,—Crazy Jane. It was the prison of the widow of Philip IV. and mother of Charles II. What wonder if her life left much to be desired? With such a husband and such a son, she had no memories nor hopes.

The kings have had a long day here. They did some good in their time. But the world has outgrown them, and the people, here as elsewhere, is coming of age. This Alcazar is built more strongly than any dynasty. It will make a glorious school-house when the repairs are finished and the Republic is established, and then may both last forever!

One morning at sunrise, I crossed the ancient bridge of Alcantara, and climbed the steep hill east of the river to the ruined castle of San Cervantes, perched on a high, bold rock, which guards the river and overlooks the valley. Near as it is to the city, it stands entirely alone. The instinct of aggregation is so powerful in this people that the old towns have no environs, no houses sprinkled in the outlying country, like modern cities. Every one must be huddled inside the walls. If a solitary house, like this castle, is built without, it must be in itself an impregnable fortress. This fine old ruin, in obedience to this instinct of jealous distrust, has but one entrance, and that so narrow that Sir John Falstaff would have been embarrassed to accept its hospitalities. In the shade of the broken walls, grass-grown and gay with scattered poppies, I looked at Toledo, fresh and clear in the early day. On the extreme right lay the new spick-and-span bull-ring, then the great hospice and Chapel of St. John the Baptist, the Convent of the Immaculate Conception, and next, the Latin cross of the Chapel of Santa Cruz, whose beautiful façade lay soft in shadow; the huge arrogant bulk of the Alcazar loomed squarely before me, hiding half the view; to the left glittered the slender spire of the Cathedral, holding up in the pure air that emblem of august resignation, the triple crown of thorns; then a crowd of cupolas, ending at last near the river-banks with the sharp angular mass of San Cristobal. The field of vision was filled with churches and chapels, with the palaces of the king and the monk. Behind me the waste lands went rolling away untilled to the brown Toledo mountains. Below, the vigorous current of the Tagus brawled over its rocky bed, and the distant valley showed in its deep rich green what vitality there was in those waters if they were only used.

A quiet, as of a plague-stricken city, lay on Toledo. A few mules wound up the splendid roads with baskets of vegetables. A few listless fishermen were preparing their lines. The chimes of sleepy bells floated softly out on the morning air. They seemed like the requiem of municipal life and activity slain centuries ago by the crozier and the crown.

Thank Heaven, that double despotism is wounded to death. As Chesterfield predicted, before the first muttering of the thunders of '89, "the trades of king and priest have lost half their value." With the decay of this unrighteous power, the false, unwholesome activity it fostered has also disappeared. There must be years of toil and leanness, years perhaps of struggle and misery, before the new genuine life of the people springs up from beneath the dead and withered rubbish of temporal and spiritual tyranny. Freedom is an angel whose blessing is gained by wrestling.

THE ESCORIAL

The only battle in which Philip II. was ever engaged was that of St. Quentin, and the only part he took in that memorable fight was to listen to the thunder of the captains and the shouting afar off, and pray with great unction and fervor to various saints of his acquaintance and particularly to St. Lawrence of the Gridiron, who, being the celestial officer of the day, was supposed to have unlimited authority, and to whom he was therefore profuse in vows. While Egmont and his stout Flemings were capturing the Constable Montmorency and cutting his army in pieces, this young and chivalrous monarch was beating his breast and pattering his panic-stricken prayers. As soon as the victory was won, however, he lost his nervousness, and divided the entire credit of it between himself and his saints. He had his picture painted in full armor, as he appeared that day, and sent it to his doting spouse, Bloody Mary of England. He even thought he had gained glory enough, and while his father, the emperor-monk, was fiercely asking the messenger who brought the news of victory to Yuste, "Is my son at Paris?" the prudent Philip was making a treaty of peace, by which his son Don Carlos was to marry the Princess Elizabeth of France. But Mary obligingly died at this moment, and the stricken widower thought he needed consolation more than his boy, and so married the pretty princess himself.

He always prided himself greatly on the battle of St. Quentin, and probably soon came to believe he had done yeoman service there. The childlike credulity of the people is a great temptation to kings. It is very likely that after the coup-d'etat of December, the trembling puppet who had sat shivering over his fire in the palace of the Elysee while Morny and Fleury and St. Arnaud and the rest of the cool gamblers were playing their last desperate stake on that fatal night, really persuaded himself that the work was his, and that *he* had saved society. That the fly should imagine he is moving the coach is natural enough; but that the horses, and the wooden lumbering machine, and the passengers should take it for granted that the light gilded insect is carrying them all,—there is the true miracle.

We must confess to a special fancy for Philip II. He was so true a king, so vain, so superstitious, so mean and cruel, it is probable so great a king never lived. Nothing could be more royal than the way he distributed his gratitude for the victory on St. Lawrence's day. To Count Egmont, whose splendid courage and loyalty gained him the battle, he gave ignominy and death on the scaffold; and to exhibit a gratitude to a myth which he was too mean to feel to a man, he built to San Lorenzo that stupendous mass of granite which is to-day the visible demonstration of the might and the weakness of Philip and his age.

He called it the Monastery of San Lorenzo el Real, but the nomenclature of the great has no authority with the people. It was built on a site once covered with cinder-heaps from a long abandoned iron-mine, and so it was called in common speech the Escorial. The royal seat of San Ildefonso can gain from the general public no higher name than La Granja, the Farm. The great palace of Catharine de Medici, the home of three dynasties, is simply the Tuileries, the Tile-fields. You cannot make people call the White House the Executive Mansion. A merchant named Pitti built a palace in Florence, and though kings and grand dukes have inhabited it since, it is still the Pitti. There is nothing so democratic as language. You may alter a name by trick when force is unavailing. A noble lord in Segovia, following the custom of the good old times, once murdered a Jew, and stole his house. It was a pretty residence, but the skeleton in his closet was that the stupid commons would not call it anything but "the Jew's house." He killed a few of them for it, but that did not serve. At last, by advice of his confessor, he had the facade ornamented with projecting knobs of stucco, and the work was done. It is called to this day "the knobby house."

The conscience of Philip did not permit a long delay in the accomplishment of his vow. Charles V. had charged him in his will to build a mausoleum for the kings of the Austrian race. He bound the two obligations in one, and added a third destination to the enormous pile he contemplated. It should be a palace as well as a monastery and a royal charnel-house. He chose the most appropriate spot in Spain for the erection of the most cheerless monument in existence. He had fixed his capital at Madrid because it was the dreariest town in Spain, and to envelop himself in a still profounder desolation, he built the Escorial out of sight of the city, on a bleak, bare hillside, swept by the glacial gales of the Guadarrama, parched by the vertical suns of summer, and cursed at all seasons with the curse of barrenness. Before it towers the great chain of mountains separating Old and New Castile. Behind it the chilled winds sweep down to the Madrid plateau, over rocky hillocks and involved ravines, — a scene in which probably no man ever took pleasure except the royal recluse who chose it for his home.

John Baptist of Toledo laid the corner-stone on an April day of 1563, and in the autumn of 1584 John of Herrera looked upon the finished work, so vast and so gloomy that it lay like an incubus upon the breast of earth. It is a parallelogram measuring from north to south seven hundred and forty-four feet, and five hundred and eighty feet from east to west. It is built, by order of the fantastic bigot, in the form of St. Lawrence's gridiron, the courts representing the interstices of the bars, and the towers at the corners sticking helpless in the air like the legs of the supine implement. It is composed of a clean gray granite, chiefly in the Doric order, with a severity of facade that degenerates into poverty, and defrauds the building of the effect its great bulk merits. The sheer monotonous walls are pierced with eleven thousand windows, which, though really large enough for the rooms, seem on that stupendous surface to shrink into musketry loopholes. In the centre of the parallelogram stands the great church, surmounted by its soaring dome. All around the principal building is stretched a circumscribing line of convents, in the same style of doleful yellowish-gray uniformity, so endless in extent that the inmates might easily despair of any world beyond them.

There are few scenes in the world so depressing as that which greets you as you enter into the wide court before the church, called El Templo. You are shut finally in by these iron-gray walls. The outside day has given you up. Your feet slip on the damp flags. An unhealthy fungus tinges the humid corners with a pallid green. You look in vain for any trace of human sympathy in those blank walls and that severe facade. There is a dismal attempt in that direction in the gilded garments and the painted faces of the colossal prophets and kings that are perched above the lofty doors. But they do not comfort you; they are tinselled stones, not statues.

Entering the vestibule of the church, and looking up, you observe with a sort of horror that the ceiling is of massive granite and flat. The sacristan has a story that when Philip saw this ceiling, which forms the floor of the high choir, he remonstrated against it as too audacious, and insisted on a strong pillar being built to support it. The architect complied, but when Philip came to see the improvement he burst into lamentation, as the enormous column destroyed the effect of the great altar. The canny architect, who had built the pillar of pasteboard, removed it with a touch, and his majesty was comforted. Walking forward to the edge of this shadowy vestibule, you recognize the skill and taste which presided at this unique and intelligent arrangement of the choir. If left, as usual, in the body of the church, it would have seriously impaired that solemn and simple grandeur which distinguishes this above all other temples. There is nothing to break the effect of the three great naves, divided by immense square-clustered columns, and surmounted by the vast dome that rises with all the easy majesty of a mountain more than three hundred feet from the decent black and white pavement. I know of nothing so simple and so imposing as this royal chapel, built purely for the glory of God and with no thought of mercy or consolation for human infirmity. The frescos of Luca Giordano show the attempt of a later and degenerate age to enliven with form and color the sombre dignity of this faultless pile. But there is something in the blue and vapory pictures which shows that even the unabashed Luca was not free from the impressive influence of the Escorial.

A flight of veined marble steps leads to the beautiful retable of the high altar. The screen, over ninety feet high, cost the Milanese Trezzo seven years of labor. The pictures illustrative of the life of our Lord are by Tibaldi and Zuccaro. The gilt bronze tabernacle of Trezzo and Herrera, which has been likened with the doors of the Baptistery of Florence as worthy to figure in the architecture of heaven, no longer exists. It furnished a half hour's amusement to the soldiers of France. On either side of the high altar are the oratories of the royal family, and above them are the kneeling effigies of

Charles, with his wife, daughter, and sisters, and Philip with his successive harem of wives. One of the few luxuries this fierce bigot allowed himself was that of a new widowhood every few years. There are forty other altars with pictures good and bad. The best are by the wonderful deaf-mute, Navarrete, of Logrono, and by Sanchez Coello, the favorite of Philip.

To the right of the high altar in the transept you will find, if your tastes, unlike Miss Riderhood's, run in a bony direction, the most remarkable Reliquary in the world. With the exception perhaps of Cuvier, Philip could see more in a bone than any man who ever lived. In his long life of osseous enthusiasm he collected seven thousand four hundred and twenty-one genuine relics,—whole skeletons, odd shins, teeth, toe-nails, and skulls of martyrs,—sometimes by a miracle of special grace getting duplicate skeletons of the same saint. The prime jewels of this royal collection are the grilled bones of San Lorenzo himself, bearing dim traces of his sacred gridiron.

The sacristan will show you also the retable of the miraculous wafer, which bled when trampled on by Protestant heels at Gorcum in 1525. This has always been one of the chief treasures of the Spanish crown. The devil-haunted idiot Charles II. made a sort of idol of it, building it this superb altar, consecrated "in this miracle of earth to the miracle of heaven." When the atheist Frenchmen sacked the Escorial and stripped it of silver and gold, the pious monks thought most of hiding this wonderful wafer, and when the storm passed by, the booby Ferdinand VII. restored it with much burning of candles, swinging of censers, and chiming of bells. Worthless as it is, it has done one good work in the world. It inspired the altar-picture of Claudio Coello, the last best work of the last of the great school of Spanish painters. He finished it just before he died of shame and grief at seeing Giordano, the nimble Neapolitan, emptying his buckets of paint on the ceiling of the grand staircase, where St. Lawrence and an army of martyrs go sailing with a fair wind into glory.

The great days of art in the Escorial are gone. Once in every nook and corner it concealed treasures of beauty that the world had nearly forgotten. The Perla of Raphael hung in the dark sacristy. The Cena of Titian dropped to pieces in the refectory. The Gloria, which had sunk into eclipse on the death of Charles V., was hidden here among unappreciative monks. But on the secularization of the monasteries, these superb canvases went to swell the riches of the Royal Museum. There are still enough left here, however, to vindicate the ancient fame of the collection. They are perhaps more impressive in their beauty and loneliness than if they were pranking among their kin in the glorious galleries and perfect light of that enchanted palace of Charles III. The inexhaustible old man of Cadora has the Prayer on Mount Olivet, an Ecce Homo, an Adoration of the Magi. Velazquez one of his rare scriptural pieces, Jacob and his Children. Tintoretto is rather injured at the Museo by the number and importance of his pictures left in this monkish twilight; among them is a lovely Esther, and a masterly Presentation of Christ to the People. Plenty of Giordanos and Bassanos and one or two by El Greco, with his weird plague-stricken faces, all chalk and charcoal. A sense of duty will take you into the crypt where the dead kings are sleeping in brass. This mausoleum, ordered by the great Charles, was slow in finishing. All of his line had a hand in it down to Philip IV., who completed it and gathered in the poor relics of royal mortality from many graves. The key of the vault is the stone where the priest stands when he elevates the Host in the temple above. The vault is a graceful octagon about forty feet high, with nearly the same diameter; the flickering light of your torches shows twenty-six sarcophagi, some occupied and some empty, filling the niches of the polished marble. On the right sleep the sovereigns, on the left their consorts. There is a coffin for Dona Isabel de Bourbon among the kings, and one for her amiable and lady-like husband among the queens. They were not lovely in their lives, and in their deaths they shall be divided. The quaint old church-mouse who showed me the crypt called my attention to the coffin where Maria Louisa, wife of Charles IV.,—the lady who so gallantly bestrides her war-horse, in the uniform of a colonel, in Goya's picture,—coming down those slippery steps with the sure footing of feverish insanity, during a severe illness, scratched *Luisa* with the point of her scissors and marked the sarcophagus for her own. All there was good of her is interred with her bones. Her frailties live on in scandalized history.

Twice, it is said, the coffin of the emperor has been opened by curious hands,—by Philip IV., who found the corpse of his great ancestor intact, and observed to the courtier at his elbow, "An honest body, Don Luis!" and again by the Ministers of State and Fomento in the spring of 1870, who started back aghast when the coffin-lid was lifted and disclosed the grim face of the Burgess of Ghent, just as Titian painted him,—the keen, bold face of a world-stealer.

I do not know if Philip's funeral urn was ever opened. He stayed above ground too long as it was, and it is probable that people have never cared to look upon his face again. All that was human had died out of him years before his actual demise, and death seemed not to consider it worth while to carry off a vampire. Go into the little apartment where his last days were passed; a wooden table and book-shelf, one arm-chair and two stools—the one upholstered with cloth for winter, the other with tin for summer—on which he rested his gouty leg, and a low chair for a secretary,—this was all the furniture he used. The rooms are not larger than cupboards, low and dark. The little oratory where he died looks out upon the high altar of the Temple. In a living death, as if by an awful anticipation of the common lot it was ordained that in the flesh he should know corruption, he lay waiting his summons hourly for fifty-three days. What tremendous doubts and fears must have assailed him in that endless agony! He had done more for the Church than any living man. He was the author of that sublime utterance of uncalculating bigotry, "Better not reign than reign over heretics." He had pursued error with fire and sword. He had peopled limbo with myriads of rash thinkers. He had impoverished his kingdom in Catholic wars. Yet all this had not sufficed. He lay there like a leper smitten by the hand of the God he had so zealously served. Even in his mind there was no peace. He held in his clenched hand his father's crucifix, which Charles had held in his exultant death at Yuste. Yet in his waking hours he was never free from the horrible suggestion that he had not done enough for salvation. He would start in horror from a sleep that was peopled with shapes from torment. Humanity was avenged at last.

So powerful is the influence of a great personality that in the Escorial you can think of no one but Philip II. He lived here only fourteen years, but every corridor and cloister seems to preserve the souvenir of his sombre and imperious genius. For two and a half centuries his feeble successors have trod these granite halls; but they flit through your mind pale and unsubstantial as dreams. The only tradition they preserved of their great descent was their magnificence and their bigotry. There has never been one utterance of liberty or free thought inspired by this haunted ground. The king has always been absolute here, and the monk has been the conscience-keeper of the king. The whole life of the Escorial has been unwholesomely pervaded by a flavor of holy water and burial vaults. There was enough of the repressive influence of that savage Spanish piety to spoil the freshness and vigor of a natural life, but not enough to lead the court and the courtiers to a moral walk and conversation. It was as profligate a court in reality, with all its masses and monks, as the gay and atheist circle of the Regent of Orleans. Even Philip, the Inquisitor King, did not confine his royal favor to his series of wives. A more reckless and profligate young prodigal than Don Carlos, the hope of Spain and Rome, it would be hard to find to-day at Mabille or Cre-morne. But he was a deeply religious lad for all that, and asked absolution from his confessors before attempting to put in practice his intention of killing his father. Philip, forewarned, shut him up until he died, in an edifying frame of mind, and then calmly superintended the funeral arrangements from a window of the palace. The same mingling of vice and superstition is seen in the lessening line down to our day. The last true king of the old school was Philip IV. Amid the ruins of his tumbling kingdom he lived royally here among his priests and his painters and his ladies. There was one jealous exigency of Spanish etiquette that made his favor fatal. The object of his adoration, when his errant fancy strayed to another, must go into a convent and nevermore be seen of lesser men. Madame Daunoy, who lodged at court, heard one night an august footstep in the hall and a kingly rap on the bolted door of a lady of honor. But we are happy to say she heard also the spirited reply from within, "May your grace go with God! I do not wish to be a nun!"

There is little in these frivolous lives that is worth knowing,—the long inglorious reigns of the dwindling Austrians and the parody of greater days played by the scions of Bourbon, relieved for a few creditable years by the heroic struggle of Charles III. against the hopeless decadence. You may walk for an hour through the dismal line of drawing-rooms in the cheerless palace that forms the gridiron's handle, and not a spirit is evoked from memory among all the tapestry and panelling and gilding.

The only cheerful room in this granite wilderness is the library, still in good and careful keeping. A long, beautiful room, two hundred feet of bookcases, and tasteful frescos by Tibaldi and Carducho, representing the march of the liberal sciences. Most of the older folios are bound in vellum, with their gilded edges, on which the title is stamped, turned to the front. A precious collection of old books and older manuscripts, useless to the world as the hoard of a miser. Along the wall are hung the portraits of the Escorial kings and builders. The hall is furnished with marble and porphyry tables, and elaborate glass cases display some of the curiosities of the library,—a copy of the Gospels that belonged to the Emperor Conrad, the Suabian Kurz; a richly illuminated Apocalypse; a gorgeous missal of Charles V.; a Greek Bible, which once belonged to Mrs. Phcebus's ancestor Cantacuzene; Persian and Chinese sacred books; and a Koran, which is said to be the one captured by Don Juan at Lepanto. Mr. Ford says it is spurious; Mr. Madoz says it is genuine. The ladies with whom I had the happiness to visit the library inclined to the latter opinion for two very good reasons,—the book is a very pretty one, and Mr. Madoz's head is much balder than Mr. Ford's. Wandering aimlessly through the frescoed cloisters and looking in at all the open doors, over each of which a cunning little gridiron is inlaid in the woodwork, we heard the startling and unexpected sound of boyish voices and laughter. We approached the scene of such agreeable tumult, and found the theatre of the monastery full of young students rehearsing a play for the coming holidays. A clever-looking priest was directing the drama, and one juvenile Thespis was denouncing tyrants and dying for his country in hexameters of a shrill treble. His friends were applauding more than was necessary or kind, and flourishing their wooden swords with much ferocity of action. All that is left of the once extensive establishment of the monastery is a boys' school, where some two hundred youths are trained in the humanities, and a college where an almost equal number are educated for the priesthood.

So depressing is the effect of the Escorial's gloom and its memories, that when you issue at last from its massive doors, the trim and terraced gardens seem gay and heartsome, and the bleak wild scene is full of comfort. For here at least there is light and air and boundless space. You have emerged from the twilight of the past into the present day. The sky above you bends over Paris and Cheyenne. By this light Darwin is writing, and the merchants are meeting in the Chicago Board of Trade. Just below you winds the railway which will take you in two hours to Madrid,—to the city of Philip II., where the nineteenth century has arrived; where there are five Protestant churches and fifteen hundred evangelical communicants. Our young crusader, Professor Knapp, holds night schools and day schools and prayer meetings, with an active devotion, a practical and American fervor, that is leavening a great lump of apathy and death. These Anglo-Saxon missionaries have a larger and more tolerant spirit of propaganda than has been hitherto seen. They can differ about the best shape for the cup and the platter, but they use what they find to their hand. They are giving a tangible direction and purpose to the vague impulse of reform that was stirring, before they came, in many devout hearts. A little while longer of this state of freedom and inquiry, and the shock of controversy will come, and Spain will be brought to life.

Already the signs are full of promise. The ancient barriers of superstition have already given way in many places. A Protestant can not only live in Spain, but, what was once a more important matter, he can die and be buried there. This is one of the conquests of the revolution. So delicate has been the susceptibility of the Spanish mind in regard to the pollution of its soil by heretic corpses that even Charles I. of England, when he came a-wooing to Spain, could hardly gain permission to bury his page by night in the garden of the embassy; and in later days the Prussian Minister was compelled to smuggle his dead child out of the kingdom among his luggage to give it Christian burial. Even since the days of September the clergy has fought manfully against giving sepulture to Protestants; but Rivero, alcalde of Madrid and president of the Cortes, was not inclined to waste time in dialectics, and sent a police force to protect the heretic funerals and to arrest any priest who disturbed them. There is freedom of speech and printing. The humorous journals are full of blasphemous caricatures that would be impossible out of a Catholic country, for superstition and blasphemy always run in couples. It was the Duke de Guise, commanding the pope's army at

Civitella, who cried in his rage at a rain which favored Alva, "God has turned Spaniard;" like Quashee, who burns his fetish when the weather is foul. The liberal Spanish papers overflowed with wit at the proclamation of infallibility. They announced that his holiness was now going into the lottery business with brilliant prospects of success; that he could now tell what Father Manterola had done with the thirty thousand dollars' worth of bulls he sold last year and punctually neglects to account for, and other levities of the sort, which seemed greatly relished, and which would have burned the facetious author two centuries before, and fined and imprisoned him before the fight at Alcolea. The minister having charge of the public instruction has promised to present a law for the prohibition of dogmatic doctrine in the national schools. The law of civil registry and civil marriage, after a desperate struggle in the Cortes, has gone into operation with general assent. There is a large party which actively favors the entire separation of the spiritual from the temporal power, making religion voluntary, and free, and breaking its long concubinage with the crown. The old superstition, it is true, still hangs like a malarial fog over Spain. But it is invaded by flashes and rays of progress. It cannot resist much longer the sunshine of this tolerant age.

Far up the mountain-side, in the shade of a cluster of chestnuts, is a rude block of stone, called the "King's Chair," where Philip used to sit in silent revery, watching as from an eyry the progress of the enormous work below. If you go there, you will see the same scene upon which his basilisk glance reposed,—in a changed world, the .same unchanging scene,—the stricken waste, the shaggy horror of the mountains, the fixed plain wrinkled like a frozen sea, and in the centre of the perfect picture the vast chill bulk of that granite pile, rising cold, colorless, and stupendous, as if carved from an iceberg by the hand of Northern gnomes. It is the palace of vanished royalty, the temple of a religion which is dead. There are kings and priests still, and will be for many coming years. But never again can a power exist which shall rear to the glory of the sceptre and the cowl a monument like this. It is a page of history deserving to be well pondered, for it never will be repeated. The world which Philip ruled from the foot of the Guadarrama has passed away. A new heaven and a new earth came in with the thunders of 1776 and 1789.

There will be no more Pyramids, no more Versailles, no more Escoriais. The unpublished fiat has gone forth that man is worth more than the glory of princes. The better religion of the future has no need of these massive dungeon-temples of superstition and fear. Yet there is a store of precious teachings in this mass of stone. It is one of the results of that mysterious law to which the genius of history has subjected the caprices of kings, to the end that we might not be left without a witness of the past for our warning and example,— the law which induces a judged and sentenced dynasty to build for posterity some monument of its power, which hastens and commemorates its ruin. By virtue of this law we read on the plains of Egypt the pride and the fall of the Pharaohs. Before the fagade of Versailles we see at a glance the grandeur of the Capetian kings and the necessity of the Revolution. And the most vivid picture of that fierce and gloomy religion of the sixteenth century, compounded of a base alloy of worship for an absolute king and a vengeful God, is to be found in this colossal hermitage in the flinty heart of the mountains of Castile.

A MIRACLE PLAY

In the windy month of March a sudden gloom falls upon Madrid, — the reaction after the *folie gaiete* of the Carnival. The theatres are at their gayest in February until Prince Carnival and his jolly train assault the town, and convert the temples of the drama into ball-rooms. They have not yet arrived at the wonderful expedition and despatch observed in Paris, where a half hour is enough to convert the grand opera into the masked ball. The invention of this process of flooring the orchestra flush with the stage and making a vast dancing-hall out of both is due to an ingenious courtier of the regency, bearing the great name of De Bouillon, who got much credit and a pension by it. In Madrid they take the afternoon leisurely to the transformation, and the evening's performance is of course sacrificed. So the sock and buskin, not being adapted to the cancan, yielded with February, and the theatres were closed finally on Ash Wednesday.

Going by the pleasant little theatre of Lope de Rueda, in the Calle Barquillo, I saw the office-doors open, the posters up, and an unmistakable air of animation among the loungers who mark with a seal so peculiar the entrance of places of amusement. Struck by this apparent levity in the midst of the general mortification, I went over to look at the bills and found the subject announced serious enough for the most Lenten entertainment, — Los Siete Dolores de Maria, — The Seven Sorrows of Mary, — the old mediaeval Miracle of the Life of the Saviour.

This was bringing suddenly home to me the fact that I was really in a Catholic country. I had never thought of going to Ammergau, and so, when reading of these shows, I had entertained no more hope of seeing one than of assisting at an auto-da-fe or a witch-burning. I went to the box-office to buy seats. But they were all sold. The forestallers had swept the board. I was never able to determine whether I most pitied or despised these pests of the theatre. Whenever a popular play is presented, a dozen ragged and garlic-odorous vagabonds go early in the day and buy as many of the best places as they can pay for. They hang about the door of the theatre all day, and generally manage to dispose of their purchases at an advance. But it happens very often that they are disappointed; that the play does not draw, or that the evening threatens rain, and the Spaniard is devoted to his hat. He would keep out of a revolution if it rained. So that, at the pleasant hour when the orchestra are giving the last tweak to the key of their fiddles, you may see these woebegone wretches rushing distractedly from the Piamonte to the Alcala, offering their tickets at a price which falls rapidly from double to even, and tumbles headlong to half-price at the first note of the opening overture. When I see the fore-staller luxuriously basking at the office-door in the warm sunshine, and scornfully refusing to treat for less than twice the treasurer's figures, I feel a divided indignation against the nuisance and the management that permits it. But when in the evening I meet him haggard and feverish, hawking his unsold places in desperate panic on the sidewalk, I cannot but remember that probably a half dozen dirty and tawny descendants of Pelayo will eat no beans to-morrow for those unfortunate tickets, and my wrath melts, and I buy his crumpled papers, moist with the sweat of anxiety, and add a slight propina, which I fear will be spent in aguardiente to calm his shattered nerves.

This day the sky looked threatening, and my shabby hidalgo listened to reason, and sold me my places at their price and a *petit verre*.

As we entered in the evening the play had just begun. The scene was the interior of the Temple at Jerusalem, rather well done, — two ranges of superimposed porphyry columns with a good effect of oblique perspective, which is very common in the Spanish theatres. St. Simeon, in a dress suspiciously resembling that of the modern bishop, was talking with a fiery young Hebrew who turns out to be Demas, the Penitent Thief, and who is destined to play a very noticeable part in the evening's entertainment. He has received some slight from the government authorities and does not propose to submit to it. The aged and cooler-blooded Simeon advises him to do nothing rash. Here at the very outset is a most characteristic Spanish touch. You are expected to be interested in Demas, and the only crime which could appeal to the sympathies of a Castilian crowd would be one committed at the promptings of injured dignity.

There is a soft, gentle strain of music played pianissimo by the orchestra, and, surrounded by a chorus of mothers and maidens, the Virgin Mother enters with the Divine Child in her arms. The Madonna is a strapping young girl named Gutierrez, a very clever actress; and the Child has been bought in the neighboring toy-shop, a most palpable and cynical wax-doll. The doll is handed to Simeon, and the solemn ceremony of the Presentation is performed to fine and thoughtful music. St. Joseph has come in sheepishly by the flies with his inseparable staff crowned with a garland of lilies, which remain miraculously fresh during thirty years or so, and kneels at the altar, on the side opposite to Miss Gutierrez.

As the music ceases, Simeon starts as from a trance and predicts in a few rapid couplets the sufferings and the crucifixion of the child. Mary falls overwhelmed into the arms of her attendants, and Simeon exclaims, "Most blessed and most unfortunate among women! thy heart is to be pierced with Seven Sorrows, and this is the first." Demas rushes in and announces the massacre of the innocents, concluding with the appropriate reflection, "Perish the kings! always the murderers of the people." This sentiment is so much to the taste of the gamins of the paraiso that they vociferously demand an encore; but the Roman soldiers come in and commence the pleasing task of prodding the dolls in the arms of the chorus.

The next act is the Flight into Egypt. The curtain rises on a rocky ravine with a tinsel torrent in the background and a group of robbers on the stage. Gestas, the impenitent thief, stands sulky and glum in a corner, fingering his dagger as you might be sure he would, and informing himself in a growling soliloquy that his heart is consumed with envy and hate because he is not captain. The captain, one Issachar, comes in, a superbly handsome young fellow, named Mario, to my thinking the first comedian in Spain, dressed in a flashy suit of leopard hides, and announces the arrival of a stranger. Enters Demas, who says he hates the world and would fain drink its foul blood. He is made politely welcome. No! he will be captain or nothing. Issachar laughs scornfully and says *he* is in the way of that modest aspiration. But Demas speedily puts him out of the way with an Albacete knife, and becomes captain, to the profound disgust of the impenitent Gestas, who exclaims, just as the profane villains do nowadays on every well-conducted stage, "Damnation! foiled again!"

The robbers pick up their idolized leader and pitch him into the tinsel torrent. This is also extremely satisfactory to the wide-awake young Arabs of the cock-loft. The bandits disperse, and Demas indulges in some fifty lines of rhymed reflections, which are interrupted by the approach of the Holy Family, hotly pursued by the soldiery of Herod. They stop under a sycamore tree, which instantly, by very clever machinery, bends down its spreading branches and miraculously hides them from the bloodthirsty legionaries. These pass on, and Demas leads the saintly trio by a secret pass over the torrent,—the Mother and Child mounted upon an ass and St. Joseph trudging on behind with his lily-decked staff, looking all as if they were on a short leave of absence from Correggio's picture-frame.

Demas comes back, calls up his merrymen, and has a battle-royal with the enraged legionaries, which puts the critics of the gallery into a frenzy of delight and assures the success of the spectacle. The curtain falls in a gust of applause, is stormed up again, Demas comes forward and makes a neat speech, announcing the author. Que salga! roar the gods,—"Trot him out!" A shabby young cripple hobbles to the front, leaning upon a crutch, his sallow face flushed with a hectic glow of pride and pleasure. He also makes a glib speech,—I have never seen a Spaniard who could not,—disclaiming all credit for himself, but lauding the sublimity of the acting and the perfection of the scene-painting, and saying that the memory of this unmerited applause will be forever engraved upon his humble heart.

Act third, the Lost Child, or Christ in the Temple. The scene is before the Temple on a festival day, plenty of chorus-girls, music, and flowers. Demas and the impenitent Gestas and Barabbas, who, I was pleased to see, was after all a very good sort of fellow, with no more malice than you or I, were down in the city on a sort of lark, their leopard skins left in the mountains and their daggers hid under the natty costume of the Judaean dandy of the period.

Demas and Gestas have a quarrel, in which Gestas is rather roughly handled, and goes off growling like every villain, *qui se respecte,*—"I will have r-revenge." Barabbas proposes to go around to the cider-cellars, but Demas confides to him that he is enslaved by a dream of a child, who said to him, "Follow me—to Paradise;" that he had come down to Jerusalem to seek and find the mysterious infant of his vision. The jovial Barabbas seems imperfectly impressed by these transcendental fancies, and at this moment Mary comes in dressed like a Madonna of Guido Reni, and soon after St. Joseph and his staff. They ask each other where is the Child,—a scene of alarm and bustle, which ends by the door of the Temple flying open and discovering, shrined in ineffable light, Jesus teaching the doctors.

In the fourth act, Demas meets a beautiful woman by the city gate, in the loose, graceful dress of the Hetairai, and the most wonderful luxuriance of black curls I have ever seen falling in dense masses to her knees. After a conversation of amorous banter, he gives her a golden chain, which she assumes, well pleased, and gives him her name, La Magdalena. A motley crowd of street loafers here rushed upon the scene, and I am sure there was no one of Northern blood in the theatre that did not shudder for an instant at the startling apparition that formed the central figure of the group. The world has long ago agreed upon a typical face and figure for the Saviour of men; it has been repeated on myriads of canvases and reproduced in thousands of statues, till there is scarcely a man living that does not have the same image of the Redeemer in his mind. Well, that image walked quietly upon the stage, so perfect in make-up that you longed for some error to break the terrible vraisemblance. I was really relieved when the august appearance spoke, and I recognized the voice of a young actor named Morales, a clever light comedian of the Bressant type.

The Magdalene is soon converted by the preaching of the Nazarene Prophet, and the scene closes by the triumphant entry into Jerusalem amid the waving of palm-branches, the strewing of flowers, and "sonorous metal blowing martial sounds." The pathetic and sublime lament, "Jerusalem! Jerusalem! thou that killest the prophets!" was delivered with great 'feeling and power.

The next act brings us before the judgment-seat of Pontius Pilate. This act is almost solely horrible. The Magdalene in her garb of penitence comes in to beg the release of Jesus of Nazareth. Pontius, who is represented as a gallant old gentleman, says he can refuse nothing to a lady. The prisoner is dragged in by two ferocious ruffians, who beat and buffet him with absurd and exaggerated violence. There is nothing more hideous than the awful concreteness of this show,—the naked helplessness of the prisoner, his horrible, cringing, overdone humility, the coarse kicking and cuffing of the deputy sheriffs. The Prophet is stripped and scourged at the pillar until he drops from exhaustion. He is dragged anew before Pilate and examined, but his only word is, "Thou hast said." The scene lasts nearly an hour. The theatre was full of sobbing women and children. At every fresh brutality I could hear the weeping spectators say, "Pobre Jesus!" "How wicked they are!" The bulk of the audience was of people who do not often go to theatres. They looked upon the revolting scene as a real and living fact. One hard-featured man near me clenched his fists and cursed the cruel guards. A pale, delicate-featured girl who was leaning out of her box, with her brown eyes, dilated with horror, fixed upon the scene, suddenly shrieked as a Roman soldier struck the unresisting Saviour, and fell back fainting in the arms of her friends.

The Nazarene Prophet was condemned at last. Gestas gives evidence against him, and also delivers Demas to the law, but is himself denounced, and shares their sentence. The crowd howled with exultation, and Pilate washed his hands in impotent rage and remorse. The curtain came down leaving the uncultivated portion of the audience in the frame of mind in which their ancestors a few centuries earlier would have gone from the theatre determined to serve God and relieve their feelings by killing the first Jew they could find. The diversion was all the better, because safer, if they happened to the good luck of meeting a Hebrew woman or child.

The Calle de Amargura—the Street of Bitterness—was the next scene. First came a long procession of official Romans,—lictors and swordsmen, and the heralds announcing the day's business. Demas appears, dragged along with vicious jerks to execution. The Saviour follows, and falls under the weight of the cross before the footlights. Another long and dreary scene takes place, of brutalities from the

Roman soldiers, the ringleader of whom is a sanguinary Andalusian ingeniously encased in a tin barrel, a hundred lines of rhymed sorrow from the Madonna, and a most curious scene of the Wandering Jew. This worthy, who in defiance of tradition is called Samuel, is sitting in his doorway watching the show, when the suffering Christ begs permission to rest a moment on his threshold. He says churlishly, Anda!—"Begone!" "I will go, but thou shalt go forever until I come." The Jew's feet begin to twitch convulsively, as if pulled from under him. He struggles for a moment, and at last is carried off by his legs, which are moved like those of the walking dolls with the Greek names. This odd tradition, so utterly in contradiction with the picture the Scriptures give us of the meek dignity with which the Redeemer forgave all personal injuries, has taken a singular hold upon the imaginations of all peoples. Under varying names,—-Ahasuerus, Salathiel, le Juif Errant, der ewige Jude,—his story is the delight and edification of many lands; and I have met some worthy people who stoutly insisted that they had read it in the Bible.

The sinister procession moves on. The audience, which had been somewhat cheered by the prompt and picturesque punishment inflicted upon the inhospitable Samuel, was still further exhilarated by the spectacle of the impenitent traitor Gestas, staggering under an enormous cross, his eyes and teeth glaring with abject fear, with an athletic Roman haling him up to Calvary with a new hempen halter.

A long intermission followed, devoted to putting babies to sleep,—for there were hundreds of them, wide-eyed and strong-lunged,—to smoking the hasty cigarette, to discussing the next combination of Prim or the last scandal in the gay world. The carpenters were busy behind the scenes building the mountain. When the curtain rose, it was worth waiting for. It was an admirable scene. A genuine Spanish mountain, great humpy undulations of rock and sand, gigantic cacti for all vegetation, a lurid sky behind, but not over-colored. A group of Roman soldiers in the foreground, in the rear the hill, and the executioners busily employed in nailing the three victims to their crosses. Demas was fastened first; then Gestas, who, when undressed for execution, was a superb model of a youthful Hercules. But the third cross still lay on the ground; the hammering and disputing and coming and going were horribly lifelike and real.

At last the victim is securely nailed to the wood, and the cross is slowly and clumsily lifted and falls with a shock into its socket. The soldiers *huzza.*, the fiend in the tin barrel and another in a tin hat come down to the footlights and throw dice for the raiment. "Caramba! curse my luck!" says our friend in the tin case, and the other walks off with the vestment.

The Passion begins, and lasts an interminable time. The grouping is admirable, every shifting of the crowd in the foreground produces a new and finished picture, with always the same background of the three high crosses and their agonizing burdens against that lurid sky. The impenitent Gestas curses and dies; the penitent Demas believes and receives eternal rest. The Holy Women come in and group themselves in picturesque despair at the foot of the cross. The awful drama goes on with no detail omitted,—the thirst the sponge dipped in vinegar, the cry of desolation, the spear-thrust, the giving up of the ghost. The stage-lights are lowered. A thick darkness—of crape—comes down over the sky. Horror falls on the impious multitude, and the scene is deserted save by the faithful.

The closing act opens with a fine effect of moon and stars. "Que linda luna!" sighed a young woman beside me, drying her tears, comforted by the beauty of the scene. The central cross is bathed in the full splendor that is denied the others. Joseph of Abarimathea (as he is here called) comes in with ladders and winding-sheets, and the dead Christ is taken from the cross. The Descent is managed with singular skill and genuine artistic feeling. The principal actor, who has been suspended for an hour in a most painful and constrained posture, has a corpse-like rigidity and numbness. There is one moment when you can almost imagine yourself in Antwerp, looking at that sublimest work of Rubens. The Entombment ends, and the last tableau is of the Mater Dolorosa in the Solitude. I have rarely seen an effect so simple, and yet so striking,—the darkened stage, the softened moonlight, the now Holy Rood spectral and tall against the starry sky, and the Dolorous Mother, alone in her sublime sorrow, as she will be worshipped and revered for coming aeons.

A curious observation is made by all foreigners, of the absence of the apostles from the drama. They appear from time to time, but merely as supernumeraries. One would think that the character of Judas was especially fitted for dramatic use. I spoke of this to a friend, and he said that formerly the false apostle was introduced in the play, but that the sight of him so fired the Spanish heart that not only his life, but the success of the piece was endangered. This reminds one of Mr. A. Ward's account of a high-handed outrage at "Utiky," where a young gentleman of good family stove in the wax head of "Jewdas Iscarrit," characterizing him at the same time as a "pew-serlanimous cuss."

"To see these Mysteries in their glory," continued my friend, "you should go into the small towns in the provinces, uncontaminated with railroads or unbelief. There they last several days The stage is the town, the Temple scene takes place in the church, the Judgment at the city hall, and the procession of the Via Crucis moves through all the principal streets. The leading roles are no joke,—carrying fifty kilos of wood over the mud and cobble-stones for half a day. The Judas or Gestas must be paid double for the kicks and cuffs he gets from tender-hearted spectators,—the curses he accepts willingly as a tribute to his dramatic ability. His proudest boast in the evening is Querian matarme,—'They wanted to kill me!' I once saw the hero of the drama stop before a wine-shop, sweating like rain, and positively swear by the life of the Devil, he would not carry his gallows a step farther unless he had a drink. They brought him a bottle of Valdepenas, and he drained it before resuming his way to Golgotha. Some of us laughed thoughtlessly, and narrowly escaped the knives of the orthodox ruffians who followed the procession."

The most striking fact in this species of exhibition is the evident and unquestioning faith of the audience. To all foreigners the show is at first shocking and then tedious; to the good people of Madrid it is a sermon, full of absolute truth and vivid reality. The class of persons who attend these spectacles is very different from that which you find at the Royal Theatre or the Comic Opera. They are sober, serious bourgeois, who mind their shops and go to mass regularly, and who come to the theatre only in Lent, when the gay world stays away. They would not dream of such an indiscretion as reading the Bible. Their doctrinal education consists of their catechism, the sermons of the curas, and the traditions of the Church. The miracle of St. Veronica, who, wiping the brow of the Saviour in the Street of Bitterness, finds his portrait on her handkerchief, is to them as real and reverend as if it were related by the evangelist. The spirit of inquiry which has broken so many idols, and opened such new vistas of thought for the minds of all the world, is as yet a stranger to Spain. It is the blind and fatal boast of even the best of Spaniards that their country is a unit in religious faith. Nunca se disputo en Espana, — "There has never been any discussion in Spain," — exclaims proudly an eminent Spanish writer. Spectacles like that which we have just seen were one of the elements which in a barbarous and unenlightened age contributed strongly to the consolidation of that unthinking and ardent faith which has fused the nation into one torpid and homogeneous mass of superstition. No better means could have been devised for the purpose. Leaving out of view the sublime teachings of the large and tolerant morality of Jesus, the clergy made his personality the sole object of worship and reverence. By dwelling almost exclusively upon the story of his sufferings, they excited the emotional nature of the ignorant, and left their intellects untouched and dormant. They aimed to arouse their sympathies, and when that was done, to turn their natural resentment against those whom the Church considered dangerous. To the inflamed and excited worshippers, a heretic was the enemy of the crucified Saviour, a Jew was his murderer, a Moor was his reviler. A Protestant wore to their bloodshot eyes the semblance of the torturer who had mocked and scourged the meek Redeemer, who had crowned his guileless head with thorns, who had pierced and slain him. The rack, the gibbet, and the stake were not enough to glut the pious hate this priestly trickery inspired. It was not enough that the doubter's life should go out in the blaze of the crackling fagots, but it must be loaded in eternity with the curses of the faithful.

Is there not food for earnest thought in the fact that faith in Christ, which led the Puritans across the sea to found the purest social and political system which the wit of man has yet evolved from the tangled problems of time, has dragged this great Spanish people down to a depth of hopeless apathy, from which it may take long years of civil tumult to raise them? May we not find the explanation of this strange phenomenon in the contrast of Catholic unity with Protestant diversity? "Thou that killest the prophets!"—the system to which this apostrophe can be applied is doomed. And it matters little who the prophets may be.

THE CRADLE AND THE GRAVE OF CERVANTES

In Rembrandt Peale's picture of the Court of Death a cadaverous shape lies for judgment at the foot of the throne, touching at either extremity the waters of Lethe. There is something similar in the history of the greatest of Spanish writers. No man knew, for more than a century after the death of Cervantes, the place of his birth and burial. About a hundred years ago the investigations of Rios and Pellicer established the claim of Alcala de Henares to be his native city; and last year the researches of the Spanish Academy have proved conclusively that he is buried in the Convent of the Trinitarians in Madrid. But the precise spot where he was born is only indicated by vague tradition; and the shadowy conjecture that has so long hallowed the chapel and cloisters of the Calle Cantarranas has never settled upon any one slab of their pavement.

It is, however, only the beginning and the end of this most chivalrous and genial apparition of the sixteenth century that is concealed from our view. We know where he was christened and where he died. So that there are sufficiently authentic shrines in Alcala and Madrid to satisfy the most sceptical pilgrims.

I went to Alcala one summer day, when the bare fields were brown and dry in their after-harvest nudity, and the hills that bordered the winding Henares were drab in the light and purple in the shadow. From a distance the town is one of the most imposing in Castile. It lies in the midst of a vast plain by the green water-side, and the land approach is fortified by a most impressive wall emphasized by sturdy square towers and flanking bastions. But as you come nearer you see this wall is a tradition. It is almost in ruins.

The crenellated towers are good for nothing but to sketch. A short walk from the station brings you to the gate, which is well defended by a gang of picturesque beggars, who are old enough to have sat for Murillo, and revoltingly pitiable enough to be millionaires by this time, if Castilians had the cowardly habit of sponging out disagreeable impressions with pennies. At the first charge we rushed in panic into a tobacco-shop and filled our pockets with maravedis, and thereafter faced the ragged battalion with calm.

It is a fine, handsome, and terribly lonesome town. Its streets are wide, well built, and silent v as avenues in a graveyard. On every hand there are tall and stately churches, a few palaces, and some two dozen great monasteries turning their long walls, pierced with jealous grated windows, to the grass-grown streets. In many quarters there is no sign of life, no human habitations among these morose and now empty barracks of a monkish army. Some of them have been turned into military casernes, and the bright red and blue uniforms of the Spanish officers and troopers now brighten the cloisters that used to see nothing gayer than the gowns of cord-girdled friars. A large garrison is always kept here. The convents are convenient for lodging men and horses. The fields in the vicinity produce great store of grain and alfalfa, — food for beast and rider. It is near enough to the capital to use the garrison on any sudden emergency, such as frequently happens in Peninsular politics.

The railroad that runs by Alcala has not brought with it any taint of the nineteenth century. The army is a corrupting influence, but not modern. The vice that follows the trail of armies, or sprouts, fungus-like, about the walls of barracks, is as old as war, and links the present, with its struggle for a better life, to the old mediaeval world of wrong. These trim fellows in loose trousers and embroidered jackets are the same race that fought and drank and made prompt love in Italy and Flanders and butchered the Aztecs in the name of religion three hundred years ago. They have laid off their helmets and hauberks, and use the Berdan rifle instead of the Roman spear. But they are the same careless, idle, dissolute bread-wasters now as then.

The town has not changed in the least. It has only shrunk a little. You think sometimes it must be a vacation, and that you will come again when people return. The little you see of the people is very attractive. Passing along the desolate streets, you glance in at an open door and see a most delightful cabinet picture of domestic life. All the doors in the house are open. You can see through the entry, the front room, into the cool court beyond, gay with oleanders and vines, where a group of women half dressed are sewing and spinning and cheering their souls with gossip. If you enter under pretence of asking a question, you will be received with grave courtesy, your doubts solved, and they will bid you go with God, with the quaint^ frankness of patriarchal times.

They do not seem to have been spoiled by overmuch travel. Such impressive and Oriental courtesy could not have survived the trampling feet of the great army of tourists. On our pilgrim-way to the cradle of Cervantes we came suddenly upon the superb facade of the university. This is one of the most exquisite compositions of plateresque in existence. The entire front of the central body of the building is covered with rich and tasteful ornamentation. Over the great door is an enormous escutcheon of the arms of Austria, supported by two finely carved statues,—on the one side a nearly nude warrior, on the other the New World as a feather-clad Indian woman. Still above this a fine, bold group of statuary, representing, with that reverent naivete of early art, God the Father in the work of creation. Surrounding the whole front as with a frame, and reaching to the ground on either side, is carved the knotted cord of the Franciscan monks. No description can convey the charming impression given by the harmony of proportion and the loving finish of detail everywhere seen in this beautifully preserved fagade. While we were admiring it an officer came out of the adjoining cuartel and walked by us with jingling spurs. I asked him if one could go inside. He shrugged his shoulders with a Quien sabe? indicating a doubt as profound as if I had asked him whether chignons were worn in the moon. He had never thought of anything inside. There was no wine nor pretty girls there. Why should one want to go in? We entered the cool vestibule, and were ascending the stairs to the first court, when a porter came out of his lodge and inquired our errand. We were wandering barbarians with an eye to the picturesque, and would fain see the university, if it were not unlawful. He replied, in a hushed and scholastic tone of voice, and with a succession of confidential winks that would have inspired confidence in the heart of a Talleyrand, that if our lordships would give him our cards he had no doubt he could obtain the required permission from the rector. He showed us into a dim, claustral-looking anteroom, in which, as I was told by my friend, who trifles in lost moments with the integral calculus, there were seventy-two chairs and one microscopic table.

The wall was decked with portraits of the youth of the college, all from the same artist, who probably went mad from the attempt to make fifty beardless faces look unlike each other. We sat for some time mourning over his failure, until the door opened, and not the porter, but the rector himself, a most courteous and polished gentleman in the black robe and three-cornered hat of his order, came in and graciously placed himself and the university at our disposition. We had reason to congratulate ourselves upon this good fortune. He showed us every nook and corner of the vast edifice, where the present and the past elbowed each other at every turn: here the boys' gymnasium, there the tomb of Valles; here the new patent cocks of the water-pipes, and there the tri-lingual patio where Alonso Sanchez lectured in Arabic, Greek, and Chaldean, doubtless making a choice hash of the three; the airy and graceful paraninfo, or hall of degrees, a masterpiece of Moresque architecture, with a gorgeous panelled roof, a rich profusion of plaster arabesques, and, *horresco referens,* the walls covered with a bright French paper. Our good rector groaned at this abomination, but said the Gauls had torn away the glorious carved panelling for firewood in the war of 1808, and the college was too poor to restore it. His righteous indignation waxed hot again when we came to the beautiful sculptured pulpit of the chapel, where all the delicate details are degraded by a thick coating of whitewash, which in some places has fallen away and shows the gilding of the time of the Catholic kings.

There is in this chapel a picture of the Virgin appearing to the great cardinal whom we call Ximenez and the Spaniards Cisneros, which is precious for two reasons. The portrait of Ximenez was painted from life by the nameless artist, who, it is said, came from France for the purpose, and the face of the Virgin is a portrait of Isabella the Catholic. It is a good wholesome face, such as you would expect. But the thin, powerful profile of Ximenez is very striking, with his red hair and florid tint, his curved beak, and long, nervous lips. He looks not unlike that superb portrait Raphael has left of Cardinal Medici.

This university is fragrant with the good fame of Ximenez. In the principal court there is a fine medallion of the illustrious founder and protector, as he delighted to be drawn, with a sword in one hand and a crucifix in the other, — twin brother in genius and fortune of the soldier-priest of France, the Cardinal-Duke Richelieu. On his gorgeous sarcophagus you read the arrogant epitaph with which he revenged himself for the littleness of kings and courtiers: —

"Praetextam junxi sacco, galeamque galero, Frater, dux, praesul, cardineusque pater. Quin, virtute mea junctum est diadema cucullo, Dum mihi regnanti patuit Gesperia."

By a happy chance our visit was made in a holiday time, and the students were all away. It was better that there should be perfect solitude and silence as we walked through the noble system of buildings and strove to re-create the student world of Cervantes's time. The chronicle which mentions the visit of Francis I. to Alcala, when a prisoner in Spain, says he was received by eleven thousand students. This was only twenty years before the birth of Cervantes. The world will never see again so brilliant a throng of ingenuous youth as gathered together in the great university towns in those years of vivid and impassioned greed for letters that followed the revival of learning. The romance of Oxford or Heidelberg or Harvard is tame compared with that electric life of a new-born world that wrought and flourished in Padua, Paris, and Alcala. Walking with my long-robed scholarly guide through the still, shadowy courts, under Renaissance arches and Moorish roofs, hearing him talking with enthusiasm of the glories of the past and never a word of the events of the present, in his pure, strong, guttural Castilian, no living thing in view but an occasional Franciscan gliding under the graceful arcades, it was not difficult to imagine the scenes of the intense young life which filled these noble halls in that fresh day of aspiration and hope, when this Spanish sunlight fell on the marble and the granite bright and sharp from the chisel of the builder, and the great Ximenez looked proudly on his perfect work and saw that it was good.

The twilight of superstition still hung heavily over Europe. But this was nevertheless the breaking of dawn, the herald of the fuller day of investigation and inquiry.

It was into this rosy morning of the modern world that Cervantes was ushered in the season of the falling leaves of 1547. He was born to a life of poverty and struggle and an immortality of fame. His own city did not know him while he lived, and now is only known through him. Pilgrims often come from over distant seas to breathe for one day the air that filled his baby lungs, and to muse among the scenes that shaped his earliest thoughts.

We strolled away from the university through the still lanes and squares to the Calle Mayor, the only thoroughfare of the town that yet retains some vestige of traffic. It is a fine, long street bordered by stone arcades, within which are the shops, and without which in the pleasant afternoon are the rosy and contemplative shopkeepers. It would seem a pity to disturb their dreamy repose by offering to trade; and in justice to Castilian taste and feeling I must say that nobody does it. Halfway down the street a side alley runs to the right, called Calle de Cervantes, and into this we turned to find the birthplace of the romancer. On one side was a line of squalid, quaint, gabled houses, on the other a long garden wall. We walked under the shadow of the latter and stared at the house-fronts, looking for an inscription we had heard of. We saw in sunny doorways mothers oiling into obedience the stiff horse-tail hair of their daughters. By the grated windows we caught glimpses of the black eyes and nut-brown cheeks of maidens at their needles. But we saw nothing to show which of these mansions had been honored by tradition as the residence of Roderick Cervantes.

A brisk and practical-looking man went past us.

I asked him where was the house of the poet. He smiled in a superior sort of way, and pointed to the wall above my head: "There is no such house. Some people think it once stood here, and they have placed that stone in the garden-wall to mark the spot. I believe what I see. It is all child's play anyhow, whether true or false. There is better work to be done now than to honor Cervantes. He fought for a bigot king, and died in a monk's hood."

"You think lightly of a glory of Castile."

"If we could forget all the glories of Castile it would be better for us."

"Puede ser," I assented. "Many thanks. May your grace go with God!"

"Health and fraternity!" he answered, and moved away with a step full of energy and dissent. He entered a door under an inscription, "Federal Republican Club."

Go your ways, I thought, radical brother. You are not so courteous nor so learned as the rector. But this Peninsula has need of men like you. The ages of belief have done their work for good and ill. Let us have some years of the spirit that denies, and asks for proofs. The power of the monk is broken, but the work is not yet done. The convents have been turned into barracks, which is no improvement. The ringing of spurs in the streets of Alcala is no better than the rustling of the sandalled friars. If this Republican party of yours cannot do something to free Spain from the triple curse of crown, crozier, and sabre, then Spain is in doleful case. They are at last divided, and the first two have been sorely weakened in detail. The last should be the easiest work.

The scorn of my radical friend did not prevent my copying the modest tablet on the wall: —

"Here was born Miguel de Cervantes Saavedra, author of Don Quixote. By his fame and his genius he belongs to the civilized world; by his cradle to Alcala de Henares."

There is no doubt of the truth of the latter part of this inscription. Eight Spanish towns have claimed to have given birth to Cervantes, thus beating the blind Scian by one town; every one that can show on its church records the baptism of a child so called has made its claim. Yet Alcala, who spells his name wrong, calling him Carvantes, is certainly in the right, as the names of his father, mother, brothers, and sisters are also given in its records, and all doubt is now removed from the matter by the discovery of Cervantes's manuscript statement of his captivity in Algiers and his petition for employment in America, in both of which he styles himself "Natural de Alcala de Henares."

Having examined the evidence, we considered ourselves justly entitled to all the usual emotions in visiting the church of the parish, Santa Maria la Mayor. It was evening, and from a dozen belfries in the neighborhood came the soft dreamy chime of silver-throated bells. In the little square in front of the church a few families sat in silence on the massive stone benches. A few beggars hurried by, too intent upon getting home to supper to beg. A rural and a twilight repose lay on everything. Only in the air, rosy with the level light, flew out and greeted each other those musical voices of the bells rich with the memories of all the days of Alcala. The church was not open, but we followed a sacristan in, and he seemed too feeble-minded to forbid. It is a pretty church, not large nor imposing, with a look of cosy comfort about it. Through the darkness the high altar loomed before us, dimly lighted by a few candles where the sacristans were setting up the properties for the grand mass of the morrow,—Our Lady of the Snows. There was much talk and hot discussion as to the placing of the boards and the draperies, and the image of Our Lady seemed unmoved by words unsuited to her presence. We know that every vibration of air makes its own impression on the world of matter. So that the curses of the sacristans at their work, the prayers of penitents at the altar, the wailing of breaking hearts bowed on the pavement through many years, are all recorded mysteriously, in these rocky walls. This church is the illegible history of the parish. But of all its ringing of bells, and swinging of censers, and droning of psalms, and putting on and off of goodly raiment, the only show that consecrates it for the world's pilgrimage is that humble procession that came on the 9th day of October, in the year of Grace 1547, to baptize Roderick Cervantes's youngest child. There could not be an humbler christening. Juan Pardo—John Gray—was the sponsor, and the witnesses were "Baltazar Vazquez, the sacristan, and I who baptized him and signed with my name," says Mr. Bachelor Serrano, who never dreamed he was stumbling into fame when he touched that pink face with the holy water and called the child Miguel. It is my profound conviction that Juan Pardo brought the baby himself to the church and took it home again, screaming wrathfully; Neighbor' Pardo feeling a little sheepish and mentally resolving never to do another good-natured action as long as he lived.

As for the neophyte, he could not be blamed for screaming and kicking against the new existence he was entering, if the instinct of genius gave him any hint of it. Between the font of St. Mary's and the bier at St. Ildefonso's there was scarcely an hour of joy waiting him in his long life, except that which comes from noble and earnest work.

His youth was passed in the shabby privation of a poor gentleman's house; his early talents attracted the attention of my Lord Aquaviva, the papal legate, who took him back to Rome in his service; but the high-spirited youth soon left the inglorious ease of the cardinal's house to enlist as a private soldier in the sea-war against the Turk. He fought bravely at Lepanto, where he was three times wounded and his left hand crippled. Going home for promotion, loaded with praise and kind letters from the generous bastard, Don Juan of Austria, the true son of the Emperor Charles and pretty Barbara Blumberg, he was captured with his brother by the Moors, and passed five miserable years in slavery, never for one instant submitting to his lot, but wearying his hostile fate with constant struggles. He headed a dozen attempts at flight or insurrection, and yet his thrifty owners would not kill him. They thought a man who bore letters from a prince, and who continued cock of his walk through years of servitude, would one day bring a round ransom. At last the tardy day of his redemption came, but not from the cold-hearted tyrant he had so nobly served. The matter was presented to him by Cervantes's comrades, but he would do nothing. So that Don Roderick sold his estate and his sisters sacrificed their dowry to buy the freedom of the captive brothers.

They came back to Spain still young enough to be fond of glory, and simple-hearted enough to believe in the justice of the great. They immediately joined the army and served in the war with Portugal. The elder brother made his way and got some little promotion, but Miguel got married and discharged, and wrote verses and plays, and took a small office in Seville, and moved with the Court to Valladolid; and kept his accounts badly, and was too honest to steal, and so got into jail, and grew every year poorer and wittier and better; he was a public amanuensis, a business agent, a sub-tax-gatherer, — anything to keep his lean larder garnished with scant ammunition against the wolf hunger. In these few lines you have the pitiful story of the life of the greatest of Spaniards, up to his return to Madrid in 1606, when he was nearly sixty years old.

From this point his history becomes clearer and more connected up to the time of his death. He lived in the new-built suburb, erected on the site of the gardens of the Duke of Lerma, first minister and favorite of Philip III. It was a quarter much affected by artists and men of letters, and equally so by ecclesiastics. The names of the streets indicate the traditions of piety and art that still hallow the neighborhood. Jesus Street leads you into the street of Lope de Vega. Quevedo and Saint Augustine run side by side. In the same neighborhood are the streets called Cervantes, Saint Mary, and Saint Joseph, and just round the corner are the Magdalen and the Love-of-God. The actors and artists of that day were pious and devout madcaps. They did not abound in morality, but they had of religion enough and to spare. Many of them were members of religious orders, and it is this fact which has procured us such accurate records of their history. All the events in the daily life of the religious establishments were carefully recorded, and the manuscript archives of the convents and brotherhoods of that period are rich in materials for the biographer.

There was a special reason for the sudden rise of religious brotherhoods among the laity. The great schism of England had been fully completed under Elizabeth. The devout heart of Spain was bursting under this wrong, and they could think of no way to avenge it. They would fain have roasted the whole heretical island, but the memory of the Armada was fresh in men's minds, and the great Philip was dead. There were not enough heretics in Spain to make it worth while to waste time in hunting them. Philip could say as Narvaez, on his death-bed, said to his confessor who urged him to forgive his enemies, "Bless your heart, I have none. I have killed them all." To ease their pious hearts, they formed confraternities all over Spain, for the worship of the Host. They called themselves "Unworthy Slaves of the Most Holy Sacrament." These grew at once very popular in all classes. Artisans rushed in, and wasted half their working days in processions and meetings. The severe Suarez de Figueroa speaks savagely of the crowd of Narcissuses and petits maitres (a word which is delicious in its Spanish dress of petimetres) who entered the congregations simply to flutter about the processions in brave raiment, to be admired of the multitude. But there were other more serious members,—the politicians who joined to stand well with the bigot court, and the devout believers who found comfort and edification in worship. Of this latter class was Miguel de Cervantes Saavedra, who joined the brotherhood in the street of the Olivar in 1609. He was now sixty-two years old, and somewhat infirm,—a time, as he said, when a man's salvation is no joke. From this period to the day of his death he seemed to be laboring, after the fashion of the age, to fortify his standing in the other world. He adopted the habit of the Franciscans in Alcala in 1613, and formally professed in the Third Order in 1616, three weeks before his death.

There are those who find the mirth and fun of his later works so inconsistent with these ascetic professions, that they have been led to believe Cervantes a bit of a hypocrite. But we cannot agree with such. Literature was at that time a diversion of the great, and the chief aim of the writer was to amuse. The best opinion of scholars now is that Rabelais, whose genius illustrated the preceding century, was a man of serious and severe life, whose gaulish crudeness of style and brilliant wit have been the cause of all the fables that distort his personal history.

No one can read attentively even the Quixote without seeing how powerful an influence was exerted by his religion even upon the noble and kindly soul of Cervantes. He was a blind bigot and a devoted royalist, like all the rest. The mean neglect of the Court never caused his stanch loyalty to swerve. The expulsion of the Moors, the crowning crime and madness of the reign of Philip III., found in him a hearty advocate and defender. _Non facit monachum cucullus,—_it was not his hood and girdle that made him a monk; he was thoroughly saturated with their spirit before he put them on. But he was the noblest courtier and the kindliest bigot that ever flattered or persecuted.

In 1610, the Count of Lemos, who had in his grand and distant way patronized the poet, was appointed Viceroy of Naples, and took with him to his kingdom a brilliant following of Spanish wits and scholars. He refused the petition of the greatest of them all, however, and to soften the blow gave him a small pension, which he continued during the rest of Cervantes's life. It was a mere pittance, a bone thrown to an old hound, but he took it and gnawed it with a gratitude more generous than the gift. From this time forth all his works were dedicated to the Lord of Lemos, and they form a garland more brilliant and enduring than the crown of the Spains. Only kind words to disguised fairies have ever been so munificently repaid, as this young noble's pension to the old genius.

It certainly eased somewhat his declining years. Relieving him from the necessity of earning his daily crust, it gave him leisure to complete and bring out in rapid succession the works which have made him immortal. He had published the first part of Don Quixote in the midst of his hungry poverty at Valladolid in 1605. He was then fifty-eight, and all his works that survive are posterior to that date. He built his monument from the ground up, in his old age. The Persiles and Sigis-munda, the Exemplary Novels, and that most masterly and perfect work, the Second Part of Quixote, were written by the flickering glimmer of a life burnt out.

It would be incorrect to infer that the scanty dole of his patron sustained him in comfort. Nothing more clearly proves his strait-ened circumstances than his frequent change of lodgings. Old men do not move for the love of variety. We have traced him through six streets in the last four years of his life. But a touching fact is that they are all in the same quarter. It is understood that his natural daughter and only child, Isabel de Saavedra, entered the Convent of the Trinitarian nuns in the street of Cantarranas—Singing Frogs—at some date unknown. All the shifting and changing which Cervantes made in these embarrassed years are within a small half-circle, whose centre is his grave and the cell of his child. He fluttered about that little convent like a gaunt old eagle about the cage that guards his callow young.

Like Albert Duerer, like Raphael and Van Dyck, he painted his own portrait at this time with a force and vigor of touch which leaves little to the imagination. As few people ever read the Exem-plary Novels,—more is the pity,—I will translate this passage from the Prologue:—

"He whom you see there with the aquiline face, chestnut hair, a smooth and open brow, merry eyes, a nose curved but well propor-tioned, a beard of silver which twenty years ago was of gold, long mustaches, a small mouth, not too full of teeth, seeing he has but six, and these in bad condition, a form of middle height, a lively color, rather fair than brown, somewhat round-shouldered and not too light on his feet; this is the face of the author of Galatea and of Don Quixote de la Mancha, of him who made the Voyage to Par-nassus, and other works which are straying about without the name of the owner: he is commonly called Miguel de Cervantes Saavedra."

There were, after all, compensations in this evening of life. As long as his dropsy would let him, he climbed the hilly street of the Olivar to say his prayers in the little oratory. He passed many a cheerful hour of gossip with Mother Francisca Romero, the independent superior of the Trinitarian Convent, until the time when the Supreme Council, jealous of the freedom of the good lady's life, walled up the door which led from her house to her convent and cut her off from her nuns. He sometimes dropped into the studios of Carducho and Caxes, and one of them made a sketch of him one fortunate day. He was friends with many of the easy-going Bohemians who swarmed in the quarter,—Cristobal de Mesa, Quevedo, and Mendoza, whose writings, Don Miguel says, are distinguished by the absence of all that would bring a "blush to the cheek of a young person,"—

"Por graves, puros, castos y excelentes."

In the same street where Cervantes lived and died, the great Lope de Vega passed his edifying old age. This phenomenon of incredible fecundity is one of the mysteries of that time. Few men of letters have ever won so marvellous a success in their own lives, few have been so little read after death. The inscription on Lope's house records that he is the author of two thousand comedies and twenty-one million of verses. Making all possible deductions for Spanish exaggeration, it must still be admitted that his activity and fertility of genius were prodigious. In those days a play was rarely acted more than two or three times, and he wrote nearly all that were produced in Spain. He had driven all competitors from the scene. Cervantes, when he published his collection of plays, admitted the impossibility of getting a hearing in the theatre while this "monster of nature" existed. There was a courteous acquaintance between the two great poets. They sometimes wrote sonnets to each other, and often met in the same oratories. But a grand seigneur like Frey Lope could not afford to be intimate with a shabby genius like brother Miguel. In his inmost heart he thought Don Quixote rather low, and wondered what people could see in it. Cervantes, recognizing the great gifts of De Vega, and, generously giving him his full meed of praise, saw with clearer insight than any man of his time that this deluge of prodigal and facile genius would desolate rather than fructify the drama of Spain. What a contrast in character and destiny between our dilapidated poet and his brilliant neighbor across the way! The one rich, magnificent, the poet of princes and a prince among poets, the "Phoenix of Spanish Genius," in whose ashes there is no flame of resurrection; the other, hounded through life by unmerciful disaster, and using the brief respite of age to achieve an enduring renown; the one, with his twenty millions of verses, has a great name in the history of literature; but the other, with his volume you can carry in your pocket, has caused the world to call the Castilian tongue the language of Cervantes. We will not decide which lot is the more enviable. But it seems a poet must choose. We have the high authority of Sancho for saying, —

"Para dar y tener
Seso ha menester."

He is a bright boy who can eat his cake and have it.

In some incidents of the closing scenes of these memorable lives there is a curious parallelism. Lope de Vega and Cervantes lived and died in the same street, now called the Calle de Cervantes, and were buried in the same convent of the street now called Calle de Lope de Vega. In this convent each had placed a beloved daughter, the fruit of an early and unlawful passion. Isabel de Saavedra, the child of sin and poverty, was so ignorant she could not sign her name; while Lope's daughter, the lovely and gifted Marcela de Carpio, was rich in the genius of her father and the beauty of her mother, the high-born Maria de Lujan. Cervantes's child glided from obscurity to oblivion no one knew when, and the name she assumed with her spiritual vows is lost to tradition. But the mystic espousals of the sister Marcela de San Felix to the eldest son of God—the audacious phrase is of the father and priest Frey Lope— were celebrated with princely pomp and luxury; grandees of Spain were her sponsors; the streets were invaded with carriages from the palace, the verses of the dramatist were sung in the service by the Court tenor Florian, called the "Canary of Heaven;" and the event celebrated in endless rhymes by the genteel poets of the period.

Rarely has a lovelier sacrifice been offered on the altar of superstition. The father, who had been married twice before he entered the priesthood, and who had seen the folly of errant loves without number, twitters in the most innocent way about the beauty and the charm of his child, without one thought of the crime of quenching in the gloom of the cloister the light of that rich young life. After the lapse of more than two centuries we know better than he what the world lost by that lifelong imprisonment. The Marquis of Mo-lins, director of the Spanish Academy, was shown by the ladies of the convent in this year of 1870 a volume of manuscript poems from the hand of Sor Marcela, which prove her to have been one of the most vigorous and original poets of the time. They are chiefly mystical and ecstatic, and full of the refined and spiritual voluptuousness of a devout young heart whose pulsations had never learned to beat for earthly objects. M. de Molins is preparing a volume of these manuscripts; but I am glad to present one of the seguidillas here, as an illustration of the tender and ardent fantasies of virginal passion this Christian Sappho embroidered upon the theme of her wasted prayers: —

Let them say to my Lover
That here I lie!
The thing of his pleasure,
His slave am I.

Say that I seek him
Only for love,
And welcome are tortures
My passion to prove.

Love giving gifts
Is suspicious and cold;
I have *all*, my Beloved,
When thee I hold.

Hope and devotion
The good may gain,
I am but worthy

Of passion and pain.

So noble a Lord
None serves in vain, —
For the pay of my love
Is my love's sweet pain.

I love thee, to love thee,
No more I desire,
By faith is nourished
My love's strong fire.

I kiss thy hands
When I feel their blows,
In the place of caresses
Thou givest me woes.

But in thy chastising
Is joy and peace,
O Master and Love,
Let thy blows not cease!

Thy beauty, Beloved,
With scorn is rife!
But I know that thou lovest me,
Better than life.

And because thou lovest me,
Lover of mine,
Death can but make me
Utterly thine!

I die with longing
Thy face to see;
Ah! sweet is the anguish

Of death to me!

This is a long digression, but it will be forgiven by those who feel how much of beautiful and pathetic there is in the memory of this mute nightingale dying with her passionate music all unheard in the silence and shadows. It is to me the most purely poetic association that clings about the grave of Cervantes.

This vein of mysticism in religion has been made popular by the recent canonization of Saint Theresa, the ecstatic nun of Avila. In the ceremonies that celebrated this event there were three prizes awarded for odes to the new saint. Lope de Vega was chairman of the committee of award, and Cervantes was one of the competitors. The prizes it must be admitted were very tempting: first, a silver pitcher; second, eight yards of camlet; and third, a pair of silk stockings. We hope Cervantes's poem was not the best. We would rather see him carry home the stuff for a new cloak and pourpoint, or even those very attractive silk stockings for his shrunk shank, than that silver pitcher which he was too Castilian ever to turn to any sensible use. The poems are published in a compendium of the time, without indicating the successful ones; and that of Cervantes contained these lines, which would seem hazardous in this colder age, but which then were greatly admired:—

"Breaking all bolts and bars,
Comes the Divine One, sailing from the stars,
Full in thy sight to dwell:
And those who seek him, shortening the road,
Come to thy blest abode,
And find him in thy heart or in thy cell."

The anti-climax is the poet's, and not mine.

He knew he was nearing his end, but worked desperately to retrieve the lost years of his youth, and leave the world some testimony of his powers. He was able to finish and publish the Second Part of Quixote, and to give the last touches of the file to his favorite work, the long pondered and cherished Persiles. This, he assures Count Lemos, will be either the best or the worst work ever produced by mortal man, and he quickly adds that it will not be the worst. The terrible disease gains upon him, laying its cold hand on his heart. He feels the pulsations growing slower, but bates no jot of his cheerful philosophy. "With one foot in the stirrup," he writes a last farewell of noble gratitude to the viceroy of Naples. He makes his will, commanding that his body be laid in the Convent of the Trinitarians. He had fixed his departure for Sunday, the 17th of April, but waited six days for Shakespeare, and the two greatest souls of that age went into the unknown together, on the 23d of April, 1616.

The burial of Cervantes was as humble as his christening. His bier was borne on the shoulders of four brethren of his order. The upper half of the coffin-lid was open and displayed the sharpened features to the few who cared to see them: his right hand grasped a crucifix with the grip of a soldier. Behind the grating was a sobbing nun whose name in the world was Isabel de Saavedra. But there was no scenic effort or display, such as a few years later in that same spot witnessed the laying away of the mortal part of Vega-Carpio. This is the last of Cervantes upon earth. He had fought a good fight. A long life had been devoted to his country's service. In his youth he had poured out his blood, and dragged the chains of captivity. In his age he had accomplished a work which folds in with Spanish fame the orb of the world. But he was laid in his grave like a pauper, and the spot where he lay was quickly forgotten. At that very hour a vast multitude was assisting at what the polished academician calls a "more solemn ceremony," the bearing of the Virgin of the Atocha to the Convent of San Domingo el Real, to see if peradventure pleased by the airing, she would send rain to the parching fields.

The world speedily did justice to his name. Even before his death it had begun. The gentlemen of the French embassy who came to Madrid in 1615 to arrange the royal marriages asked the chaplain of the Archbishop of Toledo in his first visit many questions of Miguel Cervantes. The chaplain happened to be a friend of the poet, and so replied, "I know him. He is old, a soldier, a gentleman, and poor." At which they wondered greatly. But after a while, when the whole civilized world had trans-lated and knew the Quixote by heart, the Spaniards began to be proud of the genius they had neglected and despised. They quote with a certain fatuity the eulogy of Montes-quieu, who says it is the only book they have; "a proposition" which

Navarrete considers "inexact," and we agree with Navarrete. He has written a good book himself. The Spaniards have very frankly accepted the judgment of the world, and although they do not read Cervantes much, they admire him greatly, and talk about him more than is amusing. The Spanish Academy has set up a pretty mural tablet on the facade of the convent which shelters the tired bones of the unlucky immortal, enjoying now their first and only repose. In the Plaza of the Cortes a fine bronze statue stands facing the Prado, catching on his chiselled curls and forehead the first rays of morning that leap over the hill of the Retiro. It is a well-poised, energetic, chivalrous figure, and Mr. Ger-mond de Lavigne has criticised it as having more of the sabreur than the savant. The objection does not seem well founded. It is not pleasant for the world to be continually reminded of its meannesses. We do not want to see Cervantes's days of poverty and struggle eternized in statues. We know that he always looked back with fondness on his campaigning days, and even in his decrepit age he called himself a soldier. If there were any period in that troubled history that could be called happy, surely it was the time when he had youth and valor and hope as the companions of his toil. It would have been a precious consolation to his cheerless age to dream that he could stand in bronze, as we hope he may stand for centuries, in the unchanging bloom of manhood, with the cloak and sword of a gentleman and soldier, bathing his Olympian brow forever in the light of all the mornings, and gazing, at evening, at the rosy reflex flushing the east,—the memory of the day and the promise of the dawn.